FIVE MINDS FOR THE
FUTURE

LEADERSHIP FOR THE COMMON GOOD

HARVARD BUSINESS SCHOOL PRESS

CENTER FOR PUBLIC LEADERSHIP
JOHN F. KENNEDY SCHOOL OF GOVERNMENT
HARVARD UNIVERSITY

The Leadership for the Common Good series represents
a partnership between Harvard Business School Press and
the Center for Public Leadership at Harvard University's
John F. Kennedy School of Government. Books in the series
aim to provoke conversations about the role of leaders in
business, government, and society, to enrich leadership theory
and enhance leadership practice, and to set the agenda for
defining effective leadership in the future.

OTHER BOOKS IN THE SERIES

Changing Minds
by Howard Gardner

Predictable Surprises
by Max H. Bazerman and
Michael D. Watkins

Bad Leadership
by Barbara Kellerman

Many Unhappy Returns
by Charles O. Rossotti

Leading Through Conflict
by Mark Gerzon

The Leaders We Need
by Michael Maccoby

Through the Labyrinth
by Alice H. Eagly and
Linda L. Carli

Followership
by Barbara Kellerman

Senior Leadership Teams
by Ruth Wageman, Debra A.
Nunes, James A. Burruss,
and J. Richard Hackman

*The Power of
Unreasonable People*
by John Elkington and
Pamela Hartigan

FIVE MINDS FOR THE
FUTURE

Howard Gardner

HARVARD BUSINESS PRESS
BOSTON, MASSACHUSETTS

Copyright 2008 Howard Gardner
All rights reserved
Printed in the United States of America
12 11 10 09   5 4 3 2

No part of this publication may be reproduced, stored in or introduced into
a retrieval system, or transmitted, in any form, or by any means (electronic,
mechanical, photocopying, recording, or otherwise), without the prior
permission of the publisher. Requests for permission should be directed to
permissions@hbsp.harvard.edu, or mailed to Permissions, Harvard Business
School Publishing, 60 Harvard Way, Boston, Massachusetts 02163.

ISBN 978-1-4221-4535-7

Library of Congress cataloging-in-publication data is available for this title.

The paper used in this publication meets the minimum requirements of the
American National Standard for Information Sciences—Permanence of Paper
for Printed Library Materials, ANSI Z39.48-1992.

For Oscar Bernard Gardner

Who embodies our futures

Contents

Acknowledgments

I gratefully acknowledge several sets of individuals and institutions who contributed in various ways to this book. The first set involves colleagues with whom I've worked for many years: associates at Harvard Project Zero, who helped me to understand the disciplined, synthesizing, and creating minds; and researchers on the GoodWork Project, who helped me to delineate the respectful and ethical minds. The second set involves publishers: Claudia Cassanova and Carme Castells at Paidos, my Spanish language publisher, first invited me to contribute *Las Cinco Mentes del Futuro* to its Asterisk series; Hollis Heimbouch, my wonderful editor at the Harvard Business School Press, championed the present work from its earliest incarnation. I want to mention, as well, her skilled and enthusiastic colleagues, Elizabeth Baldwin, Erin Brown, Daisy Hutton, Susan Minio, Zeenat Potia, Brian Surette, Sandra Topping, Christine Turnier-Vallecillo, and Jennifer Waring. Third, I am grateful to the several foundations and generous individuals who have supported the research that formed the basis of this book. Finally, I owe deep gratitude to my capable assistants Christian Hassold, Casey Metcalf, and Lindsay Pettingill; my exemplary literary agent Ike Williams and his ever-helpful associate Hope Denekamp; and my wife Ellen Winner, who always strikes an exquisite balance between critique and encouragement.

Preface to the Paperback Edition

In the two years since the first edition of *Five Minds for the Future* went to press, many things have happened in the world, stimulating questions have been raised about my claims, and some new thoughts have occurred to me as well. Issuing the paperback edition gives me a welcome opportunity to update readers on these developments.

First, I will address some frequently asked questions:

1. *What are the five minds?* The opportunity to lecture frequently about a book gives an author a chance to perfect his elevator speech. Nowadays, if asked about the five minds, I can summarize them in a half-dozen sentences or less:

- In the future, individuals who wish to thrive will need to be experts in at least one area—they will need a discipline.

- As synthesizers, they will need to be able to gather together information from disparate sources and put it together in ways that work for themselves and can be communicated to other persons.

- Because almost anything that can be formulated as rules will be done well by computers, rewards will go to creators— those who have constructed a box but can think outside it.

- The world of today and tomorrow is becoming increasingly diverse, and there is no way to cordon oneself off from this diversity. Accordingly, we must respect those who differ from us as well as those with whom we have similarities.

- Finally, as workers and as citizens, we need to be able to act ethically—to think beyond our own self-interest and to do what is right under the circumstances.

2. *How do we measure the five minds?* Almost as soon as my book appeared, I received inquiries from two primary audiences—educators and business leaders. And perhaps not surprisingly, given the world in which we live, I was asked whether I had developed a metric for each of the five minds. In truth I have not, but I hope that the following comments are responsive to this request.

We know the most about assessing the disciplined mind. Experts in nearly every discipline have developed both quantitative and more qualitative (or subjective) ways of assessing individual attainment in the discipline. And indeed, we could not legitimately teach the disciplines in the school, and award licenses or diplomas, without reasonably consensual metrics of evaluation.

Syntheses are best judged by laying out beforehand the criteria for a successful synthesis and determining, by consensus, whether those criteria have in fact been achieved. In my discussion of the writings of Wilber and Bryson in chapter 3, I provide one example of how to do this.

As I formulate it, creativity can be assessed only after the fact. An individual work or product is creative if and only if it changes the ways in which others in the relevant field think and act. Sometimes this judgment about creativity can be assessed quite rapidly (as in the case of a new movie format), but it can take years or even decades. And so, we can assess an individual's potential for achieving middle *C* or big *C* creativity only by looking at small *c* creativities that have already been achieved.

Which leaves respect and ethics. If I have the opportunity to observe persons in their customary milieu, particularly when no one is aware of my presence, I can readily determine whether an aura of respect pervades. In contrast, ethics can be assessed only if a role (professional, citizen) is characterized by a set of principles. Those charged with determining whether the principles have been upheld may then render judgments about who abides by the principles and who has crossed the line into compromised or bad work.

A friend, Patricia Graham, has made a shrewd observation. She says that those who behave ethically command our respect.

3. *Why use the word* mind? Admittedly, for a psychologist interested in mental processes, I am stretching the usual connotation of the word *mind*. One could substitute "five capacities" or "five perspectives." But the word *mind* reminds us that actions, thoughts, feelings, and behaviors are all products of our brain. If we want to nurture these capacities or change these perspectives, we will be trafficking in the operation of the mind.

4. *How does this work on* mind *relate to the* intelligences *discussed in your other writings?* In writing this book, I knew that whatever I said, some readers would want me to relate the five minds to the eight or more intelligences. I had not anticipated that readers would want to know *which* intelligences are involved in each of the five minds. While a full answer would require another book, I can state my conclusion briefly. The disciplined and creating minds can draw on any and all intelligences, depending on the area of work. Thus, whether disciplined or creative, a poet depends on linguistic intelligence, an architect on spatial intelligence, a therapist on interpersonal intelligence, and so on.

Respect and ethics clearly draw on the personal intelligences. Ethics, reflecting a more abstract way of thinking, draws as well on logical intelligence.

As for the synthesizing mind, it poses a problem for "multiple intelligences" or "MI" theory because synthesis often involves the operation of one, two, or even several intelligences. I suspect that gifted synthesizers can achieve their goals in different ways. For example, as a synthesizer, I happen to rely heavily on linguistic, logical, and naturalistic intelligences, but others may use spatial, artistic, or personal intelligences to achieve and convey their synthesis. Think of the synthesis achieved by Pablo Picasso in his all-encompassing work, *Guernica.*

5. *In your discussion of the respectful mind, you embrace some surprisingly conservative conclusions. Have you recovered your sense of civil liberties?* In preparing *Five Minds for the Future,* I surprised myself by becoming a critic of unrestricted free speech. In particular, I criticized the Danish newspapers that in 2005 published cartoons that ridiculed Islam.

I stand by that judgment. Indeed, even three years later, in 2008, there continues to be violence and destruction attendant to that publication. In an increasingly intimate and increasingly connected world, we need to bend over backwards to make sure that we do not gratuitously insult others, particularly those who have very different standards of religion, customs, publication, or humor.

At the same time, I now realize that there is no way in which the circulation of harmful, hurtful materials can be prevented. The Internet guarantees that. I would therefore revise my remarks. I suggest that we honor a distinction between the responsible press and other media forms. On blogs and Web sites, people will continue to write and publish whatever they like. But responsible news outlets (in the United States, the *New York Times* or the *Wall Street Journal*) should hold to a higher standard, not only in accuracy but also in protecting the sensibilities of various known and potential audiences.

6. *Are there new minds?* I am not yet ready to add any minds to my list, though various interesting ones have been proposed. I readily concede that this work would be enhanced by a fuller discussion of how strategic thinking, judgment, and wisdom contribute to a better future.

NEW THOUGHTS

I began the hardcover edition by giving two cheers for science, technology, and globalization. Since 2005, the costs of globalization, particularly for the more indigent parts of the world, have become increasingly clear; and even in developed countries, the risks of meltdowns in health, climate, resources, and the economy are more evident. There is no way to stop globalization. But we must be ever more vigilant to its costs and the need to maintain highly respectful and ethical standards with respect to all parties. And in the world that so honors the STEM disciplines (science, technology, engineering, and mathematics), we require extra efforts to make certain that the other fields of human knowledge and practice are not ignored.

Nearly everyone on the planet, including me, has a heightened awareness of the dangers of global warming and the part played by human consumption in climate changes. Technology wields a double-edged saw here. On the one hand, much of our consumption is tied to energy-exploiting technologies. Yet it is at least possible that some portion of the human contribution to climate change might be reduced thanks to innovative technologies.

As a citizen of the twenty-first century dedicated to a disciplined mind, I worry particularly about the arts and humanities.

There is less demand for these topics that were once seen as central to a liberal education. Parents, policymakers, and pupils are all pulled toward the professions, and particularly those that have the potential for making one wealthy (preferably quickly). Yet I believe that one cannot be a full person, let alone have a deep understanding of our world (including its epochal changes of climate), unless one is rooted as well in art, literature, and philosophy. Moreover, these should not be rewards available primarily to the harried middle-aged executive, but rather the cornerstone of education for all young persons. In the absence of a strong demand for these topics on the part of consumers, it is incumbent on those of us with influence to make sure that humanistically oriented fields are protected. By the same token, those who would hope to continue teaching literature, music, philosophy, and history need to present these topics in ways that speak to new generations and address issues of current concern, while avoiding "inside baseball" curricula that speak only to those with a professional stake in the field.

In a world that shows no signs of slowing down, no individual can rest on his or her intellectual laurels. I would now add that no organization can afford such sloth either. The future belongs to those organizations, as well as those individuals, that have made an active, lifelong commitment to continue to learn. While the phrase "learning organization" has become virtually a cliché, such entities are still rare and precious (in the sense that even those once on the right track can easily stop learning). Those individuals who can continue to learn and who can help preserve a zest for learning in organizations are at a special premium going forward.

In the study of cognition, it is generally thought that it takes ten years to master a discipline. This trek does not leave much time for multiple forms of mastery. I am now persuaded that, thanks to excellent computer pedagogy, forms of expertise can be attained more rapidly, perhaps in half the time. Also, because of shrewd scaffolding for those of us who have not yet attained fully mastery, there is hope that we will nonetheless be able to participate in a number of disciplines and to synthesize knowledge obtained therefrom.

In discussing ethics, I have emphasized that respect can begin at birth but that an ethical stance requires the abstract attitude that typically does not develop until adolescence. I'd like to reformulate this position. Even young children are parts of communities—home, school classroom, church—and such young persons can be inculcated into the ideals, attitudes, and behaviors appropriate to their roles within these communities. Indeed, sensitivity to "institutional culture"—the norms of a particular group as manifest in daily operation—is certainly within the ken of the child in the elementary school. (Alas, so is inculcation into unethical frames of mind.) And so instead of saying "wait until adolescence," I would instead argue "embed ethics in the sinews of all important institutions in which the child is involved." A vital step will have been taken toward an ethical career and responsible citizenship.

Initially I thought of synthesis as simply another academic performance—somewhere between disciplinary mastery and creating. I now appreciate that we attribute special value to those syntheses that go beyond the mechanical. A valued synthesis is not simply an algorithmic exercise. Rather, it gains power when it provides that sense of meaning, significance, and connectedness that so many seek today.

Put it another way. If synthesis simply entailed the following of rules, a well-programmed machine would suffice. But if synthesis is to respond to human concerns, to concerns not just of the moment but also concerns *sub species aeternitas*, then (as far as I am concerned) it becomes a distinctly human endeavor. I offer the suggestion that powerful synthesizing builds on the candidate intelligence that I have been studying most recently: "existential intelligence," defined as the "capacity to raise and address the largest questions." And when these questions (and candidate answers) are new ones, synthesizing blends into creating.

Please note that I have fallen short of relating synthesizing to religion or spirituality. For me, that would involve a step too far. But I am not as much bothered as I used to be if people want to relate synthesizing to the human search for the widest possible, most existential forms of meaning.

CLOSING REMARKS

When I wrote *Five Minds for the Future*, I was unaware of a recently published book by Daniel Pink called *A Whole New Mind*. Nor, in his book, does Daniel Pink mention my own work. Ignorance is never to be preferred over knowledgeability. Nonetheless, this state of affairs meant that two writers could each put forth their own views, and readers could judge the extent to which they were actually congruent or in conflict.

Pink is impressively alert to the "softer" sides of cognition—which he calls design, story, symphony, and play. While much of my work focuses on these topics, they are not particularly featured in the current book. That is because I do not consider specific areas of discipline, synthesizing, and creating; a person can choose to work in architecture, dance, or film, as well as in business, finance, or management consultancies. But I agree with Pink that those capacities that can be carried out automatically by machines, or far more cheaply in other parts of the world, will cease to be at a premium in the developed nations. And hence, the so-called "right brain" capacities will come increasingly to the fore.

My work brings out points that are ignored or minimized by Pink. Even though mastery of a discipline seems old-fashioned and "left brained," it is still vital. Those who do not have a discipline, as well as a sense of discipline, either will be without work or will work for someone who does have a discipline. Also, Pink leaves out how we behave toward others (respect) and how we carry out our roles as workers and citizens (ethical). He might respond that the new mind features "empathy" and that is true enough. Nonetheless, a person who is empathic does not necessarily behave in a desirable way. Empathy can be used to produce hurt—indeed, that is what sadism is, pleasure in the pain felt by others.

I endorse Pink's discussion of meaning. The faster the changes, the weaker the ambient religious and ideological systems, the more isolated the individual, the greater the thirst for meaning. I believe that the newly suggested link between synthesizing, on the one hand, and existential intelligence, on the other, captures Daniel Pink's interest in meaning.

Which brings me, in closing, to what I've been doing since *Five Minds for the Future* went to press. In addition to my day job of teaching, research, and attending committee meetings too numerous to enumerate, I have been working with young people, particularly in liberal arts colleges and secondary schools. My focus has been on ethics and meaning. While our best and brightest take a backseat to few in their mastery of disciplines and in their engagement with the real and the virtual worlds, too many of them lack a concern with the ethical implications of what they are doing and what they are not doing. Through voluntary seminars on the general topic "meaningful work in a meaningful life," my colleagues and I have sought to help students achieve a broader perspective on the decisions that they are making now and the implications of those decisions on their personal and professional lives going forward.

It is way too early to determine the effectiveness of these sessions (for updates, see http://www.goodworkproject.org, particularly discussions of the GoodWork toolkit). But I am learning a lot about how young persons are thinking about the future—how their minds are being prepared for the future. This immersion will contribute to my own understanding of the world in which I live and should help me to communicate with my grandson Oscar, to whom the hardcover and the paperback versions of this book are lovingly dedicated.

Cambridge, Massachusetts
October 2008

CHAPTER 1

Minds Viewed Globally

A Personal Introduction

FOR SEVERAL DECADES, as a researcher in psychology, I have been pondering the human mind. I've studied how the mind develops, how it is organized, what it's like in its fullest expanse. I've studied how people learn, how they create, how they lead, how they change the minds of other persons or their own minds. For the most part, I've been content to describe the typical operations of the mind—a daunting task in itself. But on occasion, I've also offered views about how we *should* use our minds.

In *Five Minds for the Future* I venture further. While making no claims to have a crystal ball, I concern myself here with the kinds of minds that people will need if they—if *we*—are to thrive in the world during the eras to come. The larger part of my enterprise remains descriptive—I specify the operations of the minds that we will need. But I cannot hide the fact that I am engaged as well in a "values enterprise": the minds that I describe are also the ones that I believe we *should* develop in the future.

Why the shift from description to prescription? In the interconnected world in which the vast majority of human beings now live, it is not enough to state what each individual or group needs to survive on its own turf. In the long run, it is not possible for parts of the world to thrive while others remain desperately poor and deeply frustrated. Recalling the words of Benjamin Franklin, "We must indeed all hang together, or, most assuredly, we shall all hang separately." Further, the world of the future—with its ubiquitous search engines, robots, and other computational devices—will demand capacities that until now have been mere options. To meet this new world on its own terms, we should begin to cultivate these capacities now.

As your guide, I will be wearing a number of hats. As a trained psychologist, with a background in cognitive science and neuroscience, I will draw repeatedly on what we know from a scientific perspective about the operation of the human mind and the human brain. But humans differ from other species in that we possess history as well as prehistory, hundreds and hundreds of diverse cultures and subcultures, and the possibility of informed, conscious choice; and so I will be drawing equally on history, anthropology, and other humanistic disciplines. Because I am speculating about the directions in which our society and our planet are headed, political and economic considerations loom large. And, to repeat, I balance these scholarly perspectives with a constant reminder that a description of minds cannot escape a consideration of human values.

Enough throat clearing. Time to bring onstage the five *dramatis personae* of this literary presentation. Each has been important historically; each figures to be even more crucial in the future. With these "minds," as I refer to them, a person will be well equipped to deal with what is expected, as well as what cannot be anticipated; without these minds, a person will be at the mercy of forces that he or she can't understand, let alone control. I'll describe each mind briefly; in the course of the book, I'll explain how it works and how it can be nurtured in learners across the age span.

The disciplined mind has mastered at least one way of thinking—a distinctive mode of cognition that characterizes a specific scholarly discipline, craft, or profession. Much research confirms that it takes up to ten years to master a discipline. The disciplined mind also knows how to work steadily over time to improve skill and understanding—in the vernacular, it is highly disciplined. Without at least one discipline under his belt, the individual is destined to march to someone else's tune.

The synthesizing mind takes information from disparate sources, understands and evaluates that information objectively, and puts it together in ways that make sense to the synthesizer and also to other persons. Valuable in the past, the capacity to synthesize becomes ever more crucial as information continues to mount at dizzying rates.

Building on discipline and synthesis, *the creating mind* breaks new ground. It puts forth new ideas, poses unfamiliar questions, conjures up fresh ways of thinking, arrives at unexpected answers. Ultimately, these creations must find acceptance among knowledgeable consumers. By virtue of its anchoring in territory that is not yet rule-governed, the creating mind seeks to remain at least one step ahead of even the most sophisticated computers and robots.

Recognizing that nowadays one can no longer remain within one's shell or on one's home territory, *the respectful mind* notes and welcomes differences between human individuals and between human groups, tries to understand these "others," and seeks to work effectively with them. In a world where we are all interlinked, intolerance or disrespect is no longer a viable option.

Proceeding on a level more abstract than the respectful mind, *the ethical mind* ponders the nature of one's work and the needs and desires of the society in which one lives. This mind conceptualizes how workers can serve purposes beyond self-interest and how citizens can work unselfishly to improve the lot of all. The ethical mind then acts on the basis of these analyses.

One may reasonably ask: Why these five particular minds? Could the list be readily changed or extended? My brief answer is this: the five minds just introduced are the kinds of minds that are particularly at a premium in the world of today and will be even more so tomorrow. They span both the cognitive spectrum and the human enterprise—in that sense they are comprehensive, global. We know something about how to cultivate them. Of course, there could be other candidates. In research for this book, I considered candidates ranging from the technological mind to the digital mind, the market mind to the democratic mind, the flexible mind to the emotional mind, the strategic mind to the spiritual mind. I am prepared to defend my quintet vigorously. Indeed, that is a chief burden of the rest of this book.

This may also be the place to forestall an understandable confusion. My chief claim to fame is my positing, some years ago, of a theory of multiple intelligences (MIs). According to MI theory, all human beings possess a number of relatively autonomous cognitive capabilities, each of which I designate as a separate intelligence. For various reasons people differ from one another in their profiles of intelligence, and this fact harbors significant consequences for school and the workplace. When expounding on the intelligences, I was writing as a psychologist and trying to figure out how each intelligence operates within the skull.

The five minds posited in this book are different from the eight or nine human intelligences. Rather than being distinct computational capabilities, they are better thought of as broad uses of the mind that we can cultivate at school, in professions, or at the workplace. To be sure, the five minds make use of our several intelligences: for example, respect is impossible without the exercise of interpersonal intelligences. And so, when appropriate, I will invoke MI theory. But for much of this book, I am speaking about policy rather than psychology, and, as a consequence, readers are advised to think about those minds in the manner of a policymaker, rather than a psychologist. That is, my concern is to convince you of the need to cultivate these minds and illustrate the best ways to do so, rather than to delineate specific perceptual and cognitive capacities that undergird the minds.

To put some flesh on these bones, I will get personal and say a bit about my own experiences with these kinds of minds. I write as a scholar and author in the social sciences and education, as a person who has considerable experience in the management of a research group. But the task of cultivating minds goes far beyond the charge of teachers and professors; it constitutes a major challenge to all individuals who work with other persons. And so, as I review these minds, I will comment on how they play out in other careers, notably in business and in the professions.

DISCIPLINED

Even as a young child, I loved putting words on paper, and I have continued to do so throughout my life. As a result, I have honed skills of planning, executing, critiquing, and teaching writing. I also work steadily to improve my writing, thus embodying the second meaning of the word *discipline*: training to perfect a skill.

My formal discipline is psychology, and it took me a decade to think like a psychologist. When I encounter a controversy about the human mind or human behavior, I think immediately about how to study the issue empirically, what control groups to marshal, how to analyze the data and revise my hypotheses when necessary.

Turning to management, I have many years of experience supervising teams of research assistants of various sizes, scopes, and missions—and I have the lessons and battle scars to show for it. My understanding has been enriched by observing successful and not-so-successful presidents, deans, and department chairs around the university; addressing and consulting with corporations; and studying leadership and ethics across the professions over the past fifteen years. Beyond question, both management and leadership are disciplines—

though they can be informed by scientific studies, they are better thought of as crafts. By the same token, any professional—whether she's a lawyer, an architect, an engineer—has to master the bodies of knowledge and the key procedures that entitle her to membership in the relevant guild. And all of us—scholars, corporate leaders, professionals—must continually hone our skills.

SYNTHESIZING

As a student I enjoyed reading disparate texts and learning from distinguished and distinctive lecturers; I then attempted to make sense of these sources of information, putting them together in ways that were generative, at least for me. In writing papers and preparing for tests that would be evaluated by others, I drew on this increasingly well-honed skill of synthesizing. When I began to write articles and books, the initial ones were chiefly works of synthesis: textbooks in social psychology and developmental psychology, and, perhaps more innovatively, the first book-length examination of cognitive science.[1]

Whether one is working at a university, a law firm, or a corporation, the job of the manager calls for synthesis. The manager must consider the job to be done, the various workers on hand, their current assignments and skills, and how best to execute the current priority and move on to the next one. A good manager also looks back over what has been done in the past months and tries to anticipate how best to carry out future missions. As she begins to develop new visions, communicate them to associates, and contemplate how to realize these innovations, she invades the realms of strategic leadership and creativity within the business or profession. And of course, synthesizing the current state of knowledge, incorporating new findings, and delineating new dilemmas is part and parcel of the work of any professional who wishes to remain current with her craft.

CREATING

In my scholarly career, a turning point was my publication in 1983 of *Frames of Mind: The Theory of Multiple Intelligences*.[2] At the time, I thought of this work as a synthesis of cognition from many disciplinary perspectives. In retrospect, I have come to understand that *Frames of Mind* differed from my earlier books. I was directly challenging the consensual view of intelligence and putting forth my own iconoclastic notions, which were ripe, in turn, for vigorous critiques. Since then, my scholarly work is better described as a series of attempts to break new ground—efforts at forging knowledge about creativity, leadership, and ethics—than as syntheses of existing work. Parenthetically, I might point out that this sequence is unusual. In the sciences, younger workers are more likely to achieve creative breakthroughs, while older ones typically pen syntheses.

In general, we look to leaders, rather than to managers, for examples of creativity. The transformational leader creates a compelling narrative about the missions of her organization or polity; embodies that narrative in her own life; and is able, through persuasion and personal example, to change the thoughts, feelings, and behaviors of those whom she seeks to lead.

And what of the role of creativity in the workaday life of the professional? Major creative breakthroughs are relatively rare in accounting or engineering, in law or medicine. Indeed, one does well to be suspicious of claims that a radically new method of accounting, bridge building, surgery, prosecution, or generating energy has just been devised. Increasingly, however, rewards accrue to those who fashion small but significant changes in professional practice. I would readily apply the descriptor *creative* to the individual who figures out how to audit books in a country whose laws have been changed and whose currency has been revalued three times in a year, or to the attorney who ascertains how to protect intellectual property under conditions of monetary (or political or social or technological) volatility.

RESPECTFUL AND ETHICAL

As I shift focus to the last two kinds of minds, a different set of analyses becomes appropriate. The first three kinds of minds deal primarily with cognitive forms; the last two deal with our relations to other human beings. One of the last two (respectful) is more concrete; the other (ethical) is more abstract. Also, the differences across career specializations become less important: we are dealing with how human beings—be they scientists, artists, managers, leaders, craftspeople, or professionals—think and act throughout their lives. And so, here I shall try to speak to and for all of us.

Turning to respect, whether I am (or you are) writing, researching, or managing, it is important to avoid stereotyping or caricaturing. I must try to understand other persons on their own terms, make an imaginative leap when necessary, seek to convey my trust in them, and try so far as possible to make common cause with them and to be worthy of their trust. This stance does not mean that I ignore my own beliefs, nor that I necessarily accept or pardon all that I encounter. (Respect does not entail a "pass" for terrorists.) But I am obliged to make the effort, and not merely to assume that what I had once believed on the basis of scattered impressions is necessarily true. Such humility may in turn engender positive responses in others.

As I use the term, *ethics* also relates to other persons, but in a more abstract way. In taking ethical stances, an individual tries to understand his or her role as a worker and his or her role as a citizen of a region, a nation, and the planet. In my own case, I ask: What are my obligations as a scientific researcher, a writer, a manager, a leader? If I were sitting on the other side of the table, if I occupied a different niche in society, what would I have the right to expect from those "others" who research, write, manage, lead? And, to take an even wider perspective, what kind of a world would I like to live in, if, to use John Rawls's phrase, I were cloaked in a "veil of ignorance" with respect to my ultimate position in the world?[3] What is my responsibility in bringing such a world into being? Every reader should be able to pose, if not answer, the same set of questions with respect to his or her occupational and civic niche.

For more than a decade, I have been engaged in a large-scale study of "good work"—work that is excellent, ethical, and engaging for the participants. In the latter part of the book I draw on those studies in my accounts of the respectful and the ethical minds.

EDUCATION IN THE LARGE

When one speaks of cultivating certain kinds of minds, the most immediate frame of reference is that of education. In many ways, this frame is appropriate: after all, designated educators and licensed educational institutions bear the most evident burden in the identification and training of young minds. But we must immediately expand our vision beyond standard educational institutions. In our cultures of today—and of tomorrow—parents, peers, and media play roles at least as significant as do authorized teachers and formal schools. More and more parents "homeschool" or rely on various extra-scholastic mentors or tutors. Moreover, if any cliché of recent years rings true, it is the acknowledgment that education must be lifelong. Those at the workplace are charged with selecting individuals who appear to possess the right kinds of knowledge, skills, minds—in my terms, they should be searching for individuals who possess disciplined, synthesizing, creating, respectful, and ethical minds. But, equally, managers and leaders, directors and deans and presidents, must continue perennially to develop all five kinds of minds in themselves and—equally—in those for whom they bear responsibility.

And so, this book should be read from a dual perspective. We should be concerned with how to nurture these minds in the younger generation, those who are being educated currently to become the leaders of tomorrow. But we should be equally concerned with those in today's workplace: how best can we mobilize our skills—and those of our coworkers—so that all of us will remain current tomorrow and the day after tomorrow?

THE OLD AND THE NEW IN EDUCATION

Let me turn now to education in the formal sense. For the most part, education has been quite conservative. This is not necessarily a bad thing. Educators have consolidated a massive amount of practical knowledge over the past centuries. I remember a conversation twenty years ago with a professor of psychology in China. I had felt that her college class, a simple recitation by one student after another of the seven laws of human memory, was largely a waste of time. With the aid of an interpreter, we talked for ten minutes about the pros and cons of different pedagogies. In the end my Chinese colleague cut off the discussion with these words: "We have been doing it this way for so long that we *know* it is right."

I discern two legitimate reasons for undertaking new educational practices. The first reason is that current practices are not actually working. We might *think*, for example, that we are educating young persons who are literate, or immersed in the arts, or capable in scientific theorizing, or tolerant of immigrants, or skilled in conflict resolution. But if evidence accrues that we are not successful in these pursuits, then we should consider altering our practices . . . or our goals.

The second reason is that conditions in the world are changing significantly. Consequent upon these changes, certain goals, capacities, and practices might no longer be indicated, or might even come to be seen as counterproductive. For example, before the invention of the printing press, when books were scarce, it was vital for individuals to cultivate a faithful and capacious verbal memory. Now that books (and notebook-sized search engines) are readily available, this goal—and the attendant mnemonic practices—are no longer at a premium. On the other hand, the ability to survey huge bodies of information—print and electronic—and to organize that information in useful ways looms more important than ever. Changing conditions may also call for new educational aspirations: for example, when no group can remain isolated from the rest of the world, respect for those of a different background and appearance becomes vital, even essential, rather than simply a polite option. Whether in charge of a classroom, a club, or a corporation, we need constantly to consider which minds are crucial, which to prioritize, and how to combine them within a single organization, as well as within a single skull.

At the start of the third millennium, we live at a time of vast changes—changes seemingly so epochal that they may well dwarf those experienced in earlier eras. In shorthand, we can speak about these changes as entailing the power of science and technology and the inexorability of globalization (the second meaning of *global* in the subtitle of this chapter). These changes call for new educational forms and processes. The minds of learners must be fashioned and stretched in five ways that have not been crucial—or *not as crucial*—until now. How prescient were the words of Winston Churchill: "The empires of the future will be empires of the mind."[4] We must recognize what is called for in this new world—even as we hold on to certain perennial skills and values that may be at risk.

SCIENCE AND TECHNOLOGY

Modern science began during the European Renaissance. Consider, first, the experiments and theorizing about the physical world. The

insights into motion and the structure of the universe that we associate with Galileo Galilei, and the understandings of light and gravity that emanated from Isaac Newton, created a body of knowledge
that continues to accumulate at an ever accelerating rate. In the biological sciences, a similar trend has occurred in the past 150 years,
building on Charles Darwin's formulations about evolution and the
ensuing discoveries of Gregor Mendel, James Watson, and Francis
Crick in genetics. While slight differences may obtain in how these
sciences are practiced across different labs, countries, or continents,
essentially there is only one mathematics, one physics, one chemistry, one biology. (I'd like to add "one psychology," but I'm not as
certain about that claim.)

Unlike science, technology did not have to wait on the specific
discoveries, concepts, and mathematical equations of the past five
hundred years. Indeed, that is precisely why in many respects the
China of 1500 seemed more advanced than its European or Middle Eastern counterparts. One can fashion perfectly functional
(even exquisite) writing implements, clocks, gunpowder, compasses,
or medical treatments even in the absence of cogent scientific theories or well-controlled experiments. Once science has taken off,
however, its link to technology becomes much tighter. It is barely
conceivable that we could have nuclear weapons, nuclear power
plants, supersonic airplanes, computers, lasers, or a medley of effective medical and surgical interventions in the absence of the sciences
of our epoch. Those societies that lack science must either remain
deprived of technological innovations or simply copy them from
societies that have developed them.

The undoubted hegemony of science and technology creates
new demands. Young people must learn to think scientifically if they
are to be able to understand and participate in the modern world.
Without understanding the scientific method, citizens cannot make
reasonable decisions about which medical course to follow when
confronted with a set of options or how to evaluate competing
claims about child rearing, psychotherapy, genetic testing, or treat-

ment of the elderly. Without having some mastery of computers, citizens cannot access the information that they need, let alone be able to use it productively, synthesize it revealingly, or challenge it knowledgeably. And needless to say, in the absence of some mastery of science and technology, individuals can scarcely hope to contribute to the continuing growth of these vital sectors. Moreover, informed opinions about controversial issues like stem cell research, nuclear power plants, genetically modified foods, or global warming presuppose a grounding in the relevant science and technology.

Having solved major mysteries about the physical and the biological worlds, scientists and technologists have more recently turned their attention to the understanding of the human mind and brain. More knowledge about psychology and neuroscience has been accrued in the past fifty years than in all prior historical eras combined. We now have well-developed, empirically based theories of intelligence, problem solving, and creativity—along with the tools, software, and hardware based (or purportedly based) on these scientific advances. Educators, professionals, managers, and leaders in business need to be cognizant of what has been established, and what may soon be established, about the nature, workings, potentials, and constraints of the human mind. Curricula developed fifty or a hundred years ago no longer suffice. But don't toss out the exquisitely evolved infant with the sudsy bathwater of earlier eras. It is easy—but dangerous—to conclude that all education in the future should simply concentrate on mathematics, science, and technology. And it is equally easy—and equally dangerous—to conclude that the forces of globalization should change everything.

THE LIMITS OF SCIENCE AND TECHNOLOGY: TWO CAVEATS

"Education is inherently and inevitably an issue of human goals and human values." I wish that this statement were mounted prominently above the desk of every policymaker. One cannot even begin to develop an educational system unless one has in mind the knowledge and skills that one values, and the kind of individuals one hopes will emerge at the end of the day. Strangely enough, however, many policymakers act as if the aims of education are self-evident; and as a consequence, when pressed, these policymakers often emerge as inarticulate, contradictory, or unbelievably prosaic. How often my eyes have glazed over as I have read vacuous proclamations about "using the mind well" or "closing the achievement gap" or "helping individuals realize their potential" or "appreciating our cultural heritage" or "having the skills to compete." Recently, in speaking to ministers of education, I've discovered a particularly Sisyphean goal: "leading the world in international comparisons of test scores." Obviously, on this criterion, only one country at a time can succeed. To state educational goals in this day and age is no easy undertaking; indeed, one purpose of this book is to posit several more gritty goals for the future.

A first caveat: science can never constitute a sufficient education. Science can never tell you what to do in class or at work. Why? What you do as a teacher or manager has to be determined by your own value system—and neither science nor technology has a built-in value system. Consider the following example. Let's say that you accept the scientific claim that it is difficult to raise psychometric intelligence (IQ). From this claim one can draw two diametrically opposite conclusions: (1) don't bother to try; (2) devote all your efforts to trying. Possibly you will succeed, and perhaps far more easily than you had anticipated. Same scientific finding: opposite pedagogical conclusions.

A second caveat, related to the first, is that science—even with engineering, technology, and mathematics thrown in—is not the only, and not even the only important, area of knowledge. (This is a trap into which many enthusiasts of globalization fall. See the collected speeches and writings of Bill Gates and Thomas Friedman, to name two gurus of our time.) Other vast areas of understanding—the social sciences, the humanities, the arts, civics, civility, ethics, health, safety, training of one's body—deserve their day in the sun, and, equally, their hours in the curriculum. Because of its current societal hegemony, the aforementioned fix on science threatens to squeeze out these other topics. Equally pernicious, many individuals feel that these other areas of knowledge ought to be approached using the same methods and constraints as does science. That this would be an enormous blunder is an understatement: What sense could we make of the greatest works of art or literature, or the most important religious or political ideas, or the most enduring puzzles about the meaning of life and death, if we only thought of them in the manner of a scientific study or proof? If all we did was quantify? What political or business leader would be credible, at a time of crisis, if all he could do was offer scientific explanations or mathematical proofs, if he could not address the hearts of his audience? The great physicist Niels Bohr once mused on this irony: "There are two kinds of truth, deep truth and shallow truth, and the function of Science is to eliminate the deep truth."

At the workplace, the same caveats prevail. While it is obviously important to monitor and take into account scientific and technological advances, the leader must have a much broader purview. Political upheavals; migrations of population; new forms of advertising, public relations, or persuasion; trends in religion or philanthropy—all of these can exert impact on an organization, be it profit or nonprofit, dispensing widgets or wisdom. A full life, like a full organization, harbors multiple disciplines. Excessive focus on science and technology reminds me of the myopia associated with ostriches or Luddites.

GLOBALIZATION

Globalization consists of a set of factors that weaken or even eliminate individual states, a process sometimes termed "deterritorialization." Historians note various periods of globalization: in earlier eras, the land mass conquered first by Alexander the Great and then, a few centuries later, by the Romans—in more recent times, the transcontinental explorations and trades of the sixteenth century, the colonization of the latter nineteenth century—are seen as instances of total or partial globalization.

Following two world wars, and a prolonged cold war, we have now embarked on what may be the ultimate, all-encompassing episode of globalization. The current incarnation features four unprecedented trends: (1) the movement of capital and other market instruments around the globe, with huge amounts circulating virtually instantaneously each day; (2) the movement of human beings across borders, with well more than 100 million immigrants scattered around the world at any time; (3) the movement of all matter of information through cyberspace, with megabytes of information of various degrees of reliability available to anyone with access to a computer; (4) the movement of popular culture—such as stylish clothing, foods, and melodies—readily, even seamlessly, across borders so that teenagers the world over look increasingly similar, even as the tastes, beliefs, and values of their elders may also converge.[5]

Needless to add, attitudes toward globalization differ enormously within and across states. Even the most vocal celebrants have been somewhat muted by recent events, such as those reflecting another global phenomenon called "stateless terrorism." But by the same token, even the most vocal critics take advantage of the undeniable accoutrements—communicating by e-mail and mobile phone, seizing on commercial symbols that are recognized the world over, holding protests in places that can be readily reached and easily monitored by diverse constituencies. While periods of retrenchment and pockets of isolationism are to be expected, it is virtually inconceivable that the four major trends just cited will be permanently stemmed.

The curricula of schools the world over may be converging, and the rhetoric of educators is certainly loaded with similar buzzwords

("world-class standards," "interdisciplinary curricula," "the knowledge economy"). Nonetheless, I believe that current formal education still prepares students primarily for the world of the past, rather
than for possible worlds of the future—Churchill's "empires of the
mind." To some extent, this actuality reflects the natural conservatism of educational institutions—a phenomenon with which I
expressed some sympathy earlier. More fundamentally, however, I
believe policymakers the world over have not come to grips ade-
quately with the major factors outlined in these pages.

To be specific: rather than stating our precepts explicitly, we
continue to assume that educational goals and values are self-evident. We acknowledge the importance of science and technology
but do not teach scientific ways of thinking, let alone how to develop individuals with the synthesizing and creative capacities essential for continual scientific and technological progress. And too
often, we think of science as the prototype of all knowledge, rather
than one powerful way of knowing that needs to be complemented
by artistic and humanistic and perhaps also spiritual stances. We acknowledge the factors of globalization—at least when they are
called to our attention—but have not figured out how to prepare
youngsters so that they can survive and thrive in a world different
from one ever known or even imagined before.

Turning to the workplace, we have become far more aware of
the necessity of continuing education. Consciousness of the five
minds is probably greater in many corporations than it is in many
school systems. Nonetheless, much of corporate education is narrowly focused on skills: innovation is outsourced to Skunk Works;
ethics is the topic of an occasional workshop. Few corporate settings embrace a liberal arts perspective, except for those executives
with the time and resources to attend a seminar at the Aspen Institute. We do not think deeply enough about the human qualities
that we want to cultivate at the workplace, so that individuals of diverse appearance and background can interact effectively with one

another. Nor do we ponder how to nurture workers who will not simply pursue their self-interest but will realize the core mission of their calling, or how to cultivate citizens who care passionately about the society in which they live and the planet that they will pass on to their successors.

I issue two—but only two—cheers for globalization. Even if the forces just cited could be handled benignly, that does not constitute a justification for ignoring or minimizing the nation, the region, and the locale. We should, for sure, think globally, but we should, for equally strong reasons, act locally, nationally, and regionally. The individual who thinks only of those at distant sites is as myopic as the individual who thinks only of those across the street or along the border. Our principal interactions will continue to be with those who live nearby, even as many of our problems and opportunities will be specific to our nation or region. As human beings, we cannot afford to sacrifice the local for the global, any more than we can afford to sacrifice the arts and humanities in our efforts to remain current with science and technology.

Earlier, I introduced the five kinds of minds that we will need to cultivate in the future, if we are to have the kinds of managers, leaders, and citizens needed to populate our planet. I hope to have made the initial case for the importance of these minds. To approach my brief sharply:

- Individuals without one or more disciplines will not be able to succeed at any demanding workplace and will be restricted to menial tasks.

- Individuals without synthesizing capabilities will be overwhelmed by information and unable to make judicious decisions about personal or professional matters.

- Individuals without creating capacities will be replaced by computers and will drive away those who do have the creative spark.

- Individuals without respect will not be worthy of respect by others and will poison the workplace and the commons.

- Individuals without ethics will yield a world devoid of decent workers and responsible citizens: none of us will want to live on that desolate planet.

No one knows precisely how to fashion an education that will yield individuals who are disciplined, synthesizing, creative, respectful, and ethical. I have argued that our survival as a planet may depend on the cultivation of this pentad of mental dispositions. Indeed, without respect, we are likely to destroy one another; without ethics, we return to a Hobbesian or Darwinian world, where the common good is nowhere to be seen. But I firmly believe that each human faculty should also be justified on noninstrumental grounds as well. As a species, we human beings have impressive positive potentials—and history is replete with individuals who exemplify one or more of these kinds of minds: the discipline of a John Keats or a Marie Curie; the synthesizing capacities of Aristotle or Goethe; the creativity of a Martha Graham or a Bill Gates; the respectful examples of those who sheltered Jews during the Second World War or who participated in commissions of truth and reconciliation during more recent decades; the ethical examples of ecologist Rachel Carson, who alerted us to the dangers of pesticides, and of statesman Jean Monnet, who helped Europe move from belligerent to peaceful institutions. Education in the broadest sense should help more human beings realize the most impressive features of the most remarkable representatives of our species.

CHAPTER 2

The Disciplined Mind

THE MOST IMPORTANT scientific discovery about learning in recent years comes from cognitive researchers who have examined
student understanding. In a typical paradigm, a secondary-school
or college student is asked to elucidate a discovery or phenomenon
with which she is not familiar but which lends itself to explanation
in terms of a concept or theory that has been already studied. The
results are surprising, consistent, and disheartening. Most students,
including those who attend our best schools and receive the highest grades, are not able to explain the phenomenon about which
they are being questioned. Even more alarmingly, many give precisely the same answer as those who have never taken the relevant
courses and have presumably never encountered the concepts relevant to a proper explanation. Using terminology that I expand on
later, these students may have accumulated plenty of factual or subject matter knowledge, but they have not learned to think in a *disciplined* manner.

Consider a few examples, deliberately drawn from different
realms of study. In physics, students continue to think of forces like

gravity or acceleration as contained within specific objects, rather than as operating in essentially equivalent fashion on all manner of entities. Asked to predict which of two objects will fall to the ground more rapidly, such students attend to the weight of the objects ("the brick is heavier than the shoe, and so it will hit the ground first"), rather than to the laws of acceleration ("absent friction, all objects accelerate at the same velocity"). In biology, either students resist the idea of evolution altogether, or they see evolution as a teleological process, with organisms guided over time by an invisible hand toward ever more perfect forms. Whether or not they have been exposed to creationist ideas or the concept of intelligent design, the idea of natural selection, as a completely unguided process, proves deeply inimical to their way of thinking. In the arts, despite exposure to contemporary forms, students continue to judge works in terms of their photographic realism, in the case of the visual arts, and in terms of simple rhyme schemes and sentimental subject matter, in the case of poetry. When asked to account for contemporary events, history students who can unravel the complex causes of past events, like World War I, fall back on simplistic unicausal explanations. "It's because of that bad guy"— whether his name happens to be Adolf Hitler, Fidel Castro, Muammar al-Qaddafi, Saddam Hussein, or Osama bin Laden. In psychology, students who have learned about the extent to which our behavior is actually determined by unconscious motivation or by external factors over which we have no control continue to magnify the power of the individual intentional agent.

Lest you think that these are isolated instances, I must emphasize that the patterns just described have been observed time and again, in subjects ranging from astronomy to zoology, from ecology to economics, and in societies all over the world. Neither Americans nor Asians nor Europeans are immune from these misconceptions. Indeed, in cases like that of biological evolution, students can be exposed to the key ideas in a number of courses and environments; yet when questioned, they cling to Lamarckian ("a giraffe's neck is long because its parent strained to reach the furthermost branch") or literal biblical ("on the fifth day . . .") accounts of the origin and evolution of species. Clearly, quite powerful forces must be at work to prevent students from thinking in a disciplinary manner.

One important contributing factor—itself drawn from evolutionary theory—can be simply stated. Human beings did not evolve over the millennia in order to have accurate explanations of the physical, biological, or social worlds. Indeed, to revert to the examples just cited, current ideas about physical forces derive principally from discoveries by Galileo, Newton, and their contemporaries, while the theory of evolution awaited the five-year voyage and the decades of reflections and synthesizing by Charles Darwin. (It's intriguing to speculate about the status of our current knowledge had those three titans never been born.) Understandings about history, the humanities, and the arts are less tied to specific times, places, and scholars, but also depend on the emergence over the centuries of sophisticated understandings on the part of the scholarly community. Such understandings might well *not* have arisen at all, or have taken different form, or may change materially in the years ahead. If one accepts evolutionary theory, it becomes clear that our existence has depended on the abilities of every one of our ancestors to survive until reproduction—nothing less, nothing more.

Moving beyond standard school subjects, we encounter the same kinds of inadequate or inappropriate thinking across the professions. Beginning law students, for example, insist on reaching a decision that is morally satisfying; this long-engrained way of thinking clashes with their teachers' insistence that decisions must be based on precedent and on process, and not on one's personal moral code. Rookie journalists prepare a coherent, well-rounded story, as if they were trying to hold the interest of a captive audience. They are unable to think backward, writing a story in such a way that it will immediately command the reader's attention while also surviving the blue pencil of the editor or the severe space limitations of the new front-page layout. The worker who has just been appointed to a managerial position attempts to retain earlier friendships as if nothing had changed; she does not understand that her new job requires that she listen, be listened to, and be respected, rather than that she win a contest of popularity or continue to exchange gossip or intimacies with former peers. The new board member fails to understand that he must now behave in a disinterested manner vis-à-vis the very CEO or president who courted him for months and then invited her to join a select, prestigious group.

In these career examples, we encounter an analogous process at work. Individuals bring to a new job the habits and beliefs that served them well before. In ordinary life, young persons are rewarded for searching for a moral solution, for relating a delicious tale at its own pace, for being a faithful friend. It does not suffice simply to advise them, "From now on, pay strict attention to precedents," or "Defend yourself against the editor's instincts to revise copy," or "Keep your distance from former associates." The old habits die hard, and the new ways of thinking and acting are hardly natural. The aspiring upwardly mobile professional must understand the reasons for these new ideas or practices; eradicate the earlier, no-longer-functional habits; and gradually consolidate a mode of behavior that is appropriate for a new position.

INSIGHTS FROM THE PAST AND THE PRESENT

For much of its relatively short history (a few thousand years), formal schooling has been characterized by its religious orientation. Teachers were typically members of a religious order; the texts to be read and mastered were holy books; and the lessons of school were moral in character. The purpose of school was to attain sufficient literacy so that one could read the sacred texts—indeed, in many cases, the ability to chant, rather than the capacity to understand or interpret, sufficed. Any talk of understanding the world—let alone adding to current understanding through further work in a discipline—would have seemed exotic. Folklore, common sense, an occasional word from the wise sufficed. (Some varieties of Islamic education still embrace this vision.)

Seven hundred years ago, in both its Chinese and its European guises, an educated elite was expected to master a set of performances. Upon completion of his education, the Confucian scholar could distinguish himself in calligraphy, archery, music, poetry, horsemanship, participation in rituals, and mastery of important texts. His counterpart in Europe was able to exhibit the performances of the trivium (grammar, rhetoric, and logic) as well as the quadrivium (music, geometry, astronomy, and arithmetic). Instead of being asked to understand and apply, the apt student would simply repeat—indeed, often memorize verbatim—the wisdom of the intellectual ancestors: Confucius or Mencius in the East; Aristotle or Aquinas in the West. Perhaps this is what that Chinese teacher of psychology, mentioned in the previous chapter, had in mind when she impatiently told me, "We have been doing it this way for so long that we *know* it is right."

Professional education, as we know it today, did not exist. To the extent that there was division of labor, individuals either learned their trade from older members of the same family—the Smiths learned to be blacksmiths from their elders—or were apprenticed to a master: "Young Jones seems to be good with his hands; he should be apprenticed to barber Cutter, so that he can learn to trim hair and lance boils." Only the ministry embraced a more formal mechanism of selection, training, and attainment of membership in the priesthood.

The Renaissance triggered a slow but inexorable change in education in the West. While a religious patina remained—and indeed continues—in many places, education became far more secular.

Nowadays, most teachers are not religiously trained, religious texts play a smaller role, and the inculcation of morality is considered the arena of family, community, and church, rather than the burden of the daily classroom. (Note that when these other institutions fail, responsibility for moral education reverts to the school. This may explain the recent emphasis on character education as pressure mounts—particularly in the United States—to allow religion into the public school classroom.) Oral recitations and written synopses continue to be valued, but there are recognitions that not all knowledge comes from the past; that knowledge is best construed as tentative; and that, particularly in the sciences, the theories and methods to be mastered will change over time.

In the last century or so, schools for the professions have mushroomed. One no longer "reads" law; one goes to law school. Medical education no longer takes place at fly-by-night trade schools—sought-after specialties can take up to ten years of formal training. Only qualified institutions can issue (or revoke) the all-important license. Increasingly, the training of managers and executives takes place at business schools and various executive education programs, with well-resourced corporations spawning their own educational facilities and tracks. So much do we take this posttertiary sector for granted that we forget how new (and controversial) it once was. Apprenticeships and mentor-ships still exist—indeed, in some ways and in some places they remain as important as ever—but they are rarely considered a substitute for formal training.

All of these educational efforts are dedicated toward the acquisition of the appropriate disciplinary knowledge, habits of minds, and patterns of behavior. Whether a student is learning general science at the beginning of adolescence, particle physics in high school, the principles of civil law at the start of law school, or the fundamentals of marketing in business school, the goal is the same: to eradicate erroneous or unproductive ways of thinking, and to put in their stead the ways of thinking and doing that mark the disciplined professional.

SUBJECT MATTER VERSUS DISCIPLINE

Why, despite the best motivated efforts, do so many students continue to adhere to erroneous or inadequate ways of thinking? A major reason, I believe, is that neither teachers nor students nor policymakers nor ordinary citizens sufficiently appreciate the differences between *subject matter* and *discipline*. Most individuals in most schools or training programs are studying subject matter. That is, like many of their teachers, they conceive their task as committing to memory a large number of facts, formulas, and figures. In science, they memorize the definitions of key terms, the formula for acceleration, the number of planets, or atomic weights, or facial nerves. In mathematics, they memorize key algebraic formulas and geometric proofs. In history, they accumulate the names and dates of key events and eras. In the arts, they know who created key works and when. In the social sciences, they learn the specifics of particular experiments and the key terms of influential theories. In law school, they master the facts of the cases. In medical school, they know the names of all the bones in the body. In business school, they fill in spreadsheets and learn to employ the terminology of sales and finance. By and large they are examined on this information: if they are good students, and have studied assiduously, they will be seen as having succeeded in their courses. And, as illustrated in Alan Bennett's play (and subsequent movie) "The History Boys," they may even succeed in gaining entrance to Oxford.[1]

Disciplines represent a radically different phenomenon. A discipline constitutes a distinctive way of thinking about the world. Scientists observe the world; come up with tentative classifications, concepts, and theories; design experiments in order to test these tentative theories; revise the theories in light of the findings; and then return, newly informed, to make further observations, redo classifications, and devise experiments. Individuals who think scientifically are aware how difficult it is to ferret out causes; they do not confuse correlation (A occurs before B) with causation (A caused B); and they are aware that any scientific consensus is subject to being overthrown, either gradually or more rapidly, in the wake of a dramatic new finding or a revolutionary theoretical paradigm.

Equivalent sketches can be given for other disciplines. For example, historians attempt to reconstruct the past from scattered and often contradictory fragments of information, mostly written, but increasingly supported by graphic, filmic, or oral testimony. Unlike science, history only happened once; it cannot be subjected to experiments or to the strict testing of rival hypotheses. Writing history is an imaginative act, which calls on the historian to place herself in remote settings and, in effect, to don the skins of the participants. Every generation necessarily rewrites history, in terms of its current needs, understandings, and available data. Scholars of literature proceed from written texts that bear only a contingent relationship to the times and events that they attempt to depict: as a dramatist, George Bernard Shaw could write equally about his own time, the era of Joan of Arc, the mythical past, or the imagined future. Literary scholars must use their tools, chief among them their own imaginations, to enter into a world of words created by an author (like Shaw) for the purpose of conveying certain meanings and achieving certain effects on readers. Historians differ on their implicit or explicit theories of the past (e.g., the Great Man Theory as opposed to the determinant role of economic, demographic, or geographic factors). By the same token, literary scholars differ in terms of the relative attention paid to the author's biography, her aesthetic intents, the literary genre employed, the historical times in which the author lived, and the historical or mythical era in which the protagonists are said to have lived.

Don't get me wrong—to study science, history, literature, indeed anything, one needs information. But shorn of their connections to one another, to underlying questions, to a disciplined way of construing this pile of information, facts are simply "inert knowledge"—

to use the pithy phrase of the British American philosopher Alfred North Whitehead. Indeed, with respect to epistemology, there is no difference between the following three statements: "The earth is 93 million miles away from the sun around which it rotates"; "The American North and South fought the Civil War for four years in the 1860s"; and "The playwright William Shakespeare portrayed the great Roman leader Julius Caesar in a play of the same name." They are simply truthful propositions. These factual statements only gain meaning by being placed in the context, respectively, of the layout of the solar system (and how that has been determined), the struggles about slavery and union that rent the American fabric for decades, and the aesthetically imaginative way in which one sixteenth-century English author re-created certain personages portrayed in Plutarch's *Lives*.

Distinctive ways of thinking characterize the professions as well and, in the happiest circumstances, are modeled by skilled practitioners. Educator Lee Shulman delineates the "signature pedagogies" of each profession.[2] In law, the teacher engages in a Socratic dialogue with students; every time a student comes up with a possible solution to a case, the teacher dredges up a counterexample until, in most cases, the student throws up her hands in confusion. In medicine, the student accompanies a senior physician on rounds, observes the recorded data on each patient as well as the interactions of the moment, and seeks to arrive at both a diagnosis and a recommended course of treatment. In design school, students sit at work areas, with physical models or digital models on a computer screen; they work together to come up with designs, and the teacher circulates among them, making occasional supportive or critical comments. In business school, students come to class prepared to discuss a multifaceted case; aware that the information is necessarily incomplete, they nonetheless have to recommend a course of action, one that might lead to the salvation, prospering, or destruction of a division or even an entire corporation. None of these pedagogical encounters captures with full fidelity what might happen on a day-to-day basis once the student becomes a professional, but these experiences are thought to constitute the best possible preparation for work. No doubt, an increasing proportion of this education will be carried out in the future via simulations or other virtual realities.

Signature pedagogies demonstrate that the life of the professional is not equivalent to the life of the young student. For these pedagogies to be effective, both students and teachers must operate on a level quite different from that typically followed in the years before professional school. That is, students must see information not as an end in itself or as a stepping-stone to more advanced types of information ("I took Algebra I to prepare for Algebra II"), but rather as a means to better-informed practice. For their parts, teachers—acting to some extent as coaches—must provide feedback on their students' abilities to pick up the distinctive habits of mind and behavior of the professional. To the extent that examinations or feedback focuses on factual information, the student may be well prepared to become a certain kind of professor, but not a practicing professional.

In this book, I say little about the traditional crafts or trades. I should stress, though, that each of these—from weaving rugs to repairing electrical circuits—entails at least one discipline. To the extent that personal service or personal touch continues to be valued, these disciplines will provide a good livelihood for those who have mastered them. But my focus here falls chiefly on the scholarly disciplines that one should acquire by the end of the adolescence, and the one or more professional disciplines needed to be a productive worker in society.

HOW TO DISCIPLINE A MIND

Over the years, teachers have fashioned ways in which to convey disciplines to young minds. Indeed, in no other way could we continue to have a steady supply of scientists, mathematicians, artists, historians, critics, lawyers, executives, managers, and other kinds of scholars and professionals. The training of disciplinarians takes place through the identification of mutual interests and gifts ("you have the talent to become a scientist/historian/literary critic/lawyer/ engineer/executive"); the modeling of ways of thinking ("here's how we go about proving a theorem of this sort"); the successful completion of certain signature assignments ("that's a good analysis of Sonnet 23; let's see whether you can carry out an analogous in- terpretation of Sonnet 36"); the provision of timely, useful feedback on earlier disciplinary efforts ("you did a pretty good job of ana- lyzing those data, but next time, think through the specifics of the control conditions more carefully before you start the experi- ment"—or, in the case of business school, "realize that the data may have been massaged so as to make a particular manager look good"); and the passing through successive hoops *en route* to be- coming a master of the discipline ("you've now learned how to write a good lead to the story; the next job is to order the para- graphs so that the important points will survive, even if the story has to be cut in half").

But most young persons are not going to enter the ranks of one specific discipline. And so educators face a choice: do not teach them the discipline at all; introduce them to the facts of the subject and let them fend for themselves; or strive at least to give them a taste—a "threshold experience" in David Perkins's term[3]—of what it is like to think in a disciplined manner.

I believe it is essential for individuals in the future to be able to think in the ways that characterize the major disciplines. At the precollegiate level, my own short list includes science, mathematics, history, and at least one art form (such as figure drawing, playing an instrument, or writing one-act plays). I choose those disciplines be- cause they are gateways: one science introduces methods used in several; a course of history opens up the gates to a range of social sciences; one art form eases entry into others. Should they lack such disciplinary acumen, students will be completely dependent on others as they attempt to formulate views about their medical options, the political scene, new works of art, economic prospects, child rearing, possible scenarios of the future, among many other topics. These forms of thinking will serve students well, no matter what profession they eventually enter. In the absence of these forms of thinking, undisciplined individuals may not even be able to ascertain *which* persons or ideas are reliable guides, informants, opinion leaders. And so they become easy game for charlatans and demagogues. Mastery of the basic skills is a necessary but not sufficient prerequisite. Knowledge of facts is a useful ornament but a fundamentally different undertaking than thinking in a discipline.

Of course, once one enters a university, a graduate school, or the workplace, the target profession determines the relevant discipline, subdiscipline, or set of disciplines. Mathematics, mechanics, and management each feature specific disciplines. Facts and figures are welcome ornaments, but the structure and processes of disciplines are the Christmas trees on which those ornaments must be hung.

How to achieve a disciplined mind? Whether one has in mind the discipline of history, law, or management, four steps are essential:

1. Identify truly important topics or concepts within the discipline. Some of these will be content—for example, the nature of gravity, the components of a civil war, the rise of the novel, the penal code of one's state, the laws of supply and demand. Some of these will be methodological: how to set up a scientific experiment; how to make sense of an original, authenticated document from the past; how to analyze a Shakespearean sonnet, a classical sonata form, a medieval triptych, a recent decision by the U.S. Supreme Court, a balance sheet.

2. Spend a significant amount of time on this topic. If it is worth studying, it is worth studying deeply, over a signifi-

cant period of time, using a variety of examples and
modes of analysis.

3. Approach the topic in a number of ways. Here is where an
education for disciplinary understanding takes advantage
of the variety of ways in which individuals can learn. Any
lesson is more likely to be understood if it has been approached through diverse entry points: these can include
stories, logical expositions, debate, dialogue, humor, role
play, graphic depictions, video or cinematic presentations,
embodiments of the lesson in question in the ideas, behaviors, and attitudes of a respected person. This is not to say
that every topic ought to be taught in three or thirty
canonical ways—but rather that any topic worth studying
is open to a plurality of approaches.

Here, by the way, is where one kind of mind—the disciplined mind—encounters my theory of multiple intelligences. While a specific discipline may prioritize one kind
of intelligence over the others, a good pedagogue will invariably draw on several intelligences in inculcating key
concepts or processes. The study of architecture may highlight spatial intelligence, but an effective teacher of architectural design may well underscore and make use of
logical, naturalist, and interpersonal perspectives.

A variety of entry points achieves two important goals.
First of all, the teacher reaches more students, because
some learn better through stories, others through debate,
works of art, or identification with a skilled practitioner.
Second, such an approach demonstrates what genuine
understanding is like. Any individual with a deep understanding of a topic or method can think about it in a variety of ways. Conversely, an individual exhibits her current
limitations when she can only conceptualize her topic in
a single way. One cannot be disciplined without such

conceptual agility. As I'll discuss in the following chapters, multiple ways of thinking about a topic are also essential for the synthesizing and the creating minds.

4. Most important, set up "performances of understanding" and give students ample opportunities to perform their understandings under a variety of conditions. We customarily think of understanding as something that occurs within the mind or brain—and of course, in a literal sense, it does. Yet neither the student nor the teacher, neither the apprentice nor the master, can ascertain whether the understanding is genuine, let alone robust, unless the student is able to mobilize that putative understanding publicly to illuminate some hitherto unfamiliar example. Both teacher and students ought to strive to perform their current understandings; much of training should consist of formative exercises, with detailed feedback on where the performance is adequate, where it falls short, why it falls short, what can be done to fine-tune the performance.

Why talk about performances of understanding? So long as we examine individuals only on problems to which they have already been exposed, we simply cannot ascertain whether they have truly understood. They *might* have understood, but it is just as likely that they are simply relying on a good memory. The only reliable way to determine whether understanding has truly been achieved is to pose a *new* question or puzzle—one on which individuals could have not been coached—and to see how they fare. Understanding the nature of a civil war does not mean knowing the dates of the nineteenth-century American or the twentieth-century Spanish struggles; it means judging whether the Vietnamese battles of the 1960s or the Rwandan conflicts of the 1990s should be considered examples of civil wars, and if not, why not. Knowing how to behave in a business crisis does not mean stating what General Motors did fifty years ago; it means having a conceptualization and procedure in place so one can act appropriately in case of a sudden spurt in illness among consumers of one's product or an unexpected decline in profits. When critics deride business schools as being too academic, they usually mean that the ultimate uses of the purveyed knowledge are not evident; students are not forced to stretch or flex their text or lecture- or discussion-obtained knowledge. Here, in brief, is why most standardized measures of learning are of little use; they do not reveal whether the student can actually make use of the classroom material—the subject matter—once she steps outside the door. And here is why traditional training in the crafts requires a culminating masterpiece before the journeyman can rise to the level of master.

To be sure, one can go too far in requiring performances of understanding. I have little sympathy with currently popular techniques of job interviews, where candidates are required to come up with putatively creative responses under conditions of stress. Unless the actual job in question requires employees to come up with ten trademarks in two minutes, or to figure out how to light a bulb using only a battery and a wire, such performances are more likely to sift out the glib than to identify the deeply disciplined or the genuinely creative.

Finally, we arrive at the explanation for the smoking-gun examples introduced at the beginning of the chapter. Students may succeed on items to which they have already been exposed; they fail when asked to explicate examples that were not, so to speak, in the textbook or the homework assignment. And so, bearing in mind these telltale examples, we ask students of physics to predict what will happen to familiar objects when they are launched into outer space initially and over a specified period of time; or we ask students of history to discourse on what might be the issues spawning a civil war in Chechnya or to explain the reasons provoking a recent terrorist attack; or we ask students of literature to analyze the poems of a recently chosen poet laureate or to critique a newly written play about Anthony and Cleopatra; or we ask medical students to outline a course of treatment for a newly discovered strain of flu; or we ask those enrolled in business school to recommend a course of action to a recently turned-around airline that has suddenly been threatened with a potentially debilitating strike. There is no need for students to respond to these challenges in the manner of a distinguished disciplinarian—that feat takes years to accomplish. But if their responses are essentially indistinguishable from those of individuals who have never studied the designated topics—if, indeed, the way that they approach the problem demonstrates little or no disciplinary method—we must then face the uncomfortable possibility that factual knowledge may have increased without a correlative increase in disciplinary sophistication.

The absence of disciplinary thinking matters. Shorn of these sophisticated ways of thinking, individuals remain essentially unschooled—no different, indeed, from uneducated individuals—in how they think of the physical world, the biological world, the world of human beings, the world of imaginative creations, the world of commerce. They have not benefited from the genuine progress achieved by learned individuals in the past few thousand years; though they may sport trendy dress and use up-to-date argot, the undisciplined students are essentially stranded in the same intellectual place as barbarians. They are not able to understand what is said about current events, new scientific discoveries or technological feats, new mathematical techniques, new works of art, new forms of financing, new environmental regulations; accordingly, they will not be able to have informed opinions about the events of the day, the year, the century. They feel alienated and stupid—or, equally bad, they feel resentment, antagonism, even hatred, vis-à-vis those who do seem to be able to perform their understandings in a disciplined manner.

But, you might retort, individuals bereft of disciplinary understanding can still get along in daily life and make a decent, perhaps even a spectacular living—and I would not dispute this riposte. (I read the celebrity magazines too—though, like you, only at the supermarket checkout counter.) Yet, I would add, such persons are then completely dependent on others when they must make decisions about their own health or welfare or vote on issues of importance for their time. Moreover, there are fewer and fewer occupations in which one can progress without at least some sophistication in scientific, mathematical, professional, commercial, and/or humanistic thinking. Scholarly disciplines allow you to participate knowledgeably in the world; professional disciplines allow you to thrive at the workplace.

Another retort: disciplinary thinking is all well and good, but—in the absence of facts, figures, other kinds of information—one can't really use it. This response also harbors some truth: we do need to know some things, and we appropriately respect individuals who have lots of knowledge at their mental fingertips. But two more important considerations trump a mountain of facts. First, in this day of search engines, ubiquitous physical and virtual encyclopedias, and increasingly powerful handheld computers, nearly all required or desired information can be retrieved almost instantaneously. Just as the book made a photographic memory a luxury, current computers render forced memorization even less important. And if one believes that it is desirable for individuals to memorize speeches or poems or melodies, such an exercise should be done for its own sake ("it's beautiful, it's satisfying"), and not for the will-o'-the-wisp goal of improving general mnemonic capacity.

Second, in the course of acquiring a disciplined approach to consequential topics, individuals will indeed pick up useful information: the relative positions and distances of the other planets, the important figures and events of a civil war, the literary devices used by Shakespeare or Pirandello to create powerful characters and dramatic tension, the organizational charts of major corporations and the identities of those who inhabit them. Moreover, this "core knowledge" or "cultural literacy" will be both more entrenched *and* more flexible because it has been acquired in a meaningful context; it is not merely part of a forced regimen of committing someone else's list to memory.

In the end there remains a far more important reason for disciplinary understanding. That is because, like the most salient experiences of life (from orgasm to philanthropy), its achievement breeds a desire for more. Once one has understood well a particular play, a particular war, a particular physical or biological or managerial concept, the appetite has been whetted for additional and deeper understanding, and for clear-cut performances in which one's understanding can be demonstrated to others and to oneself. Indeed, the genuine understander is unlikely in the future to accept only superficial understandings. Rather, having eaten from the tree of understanding, he or she is likely to return there repeatedly for ever more satisfying intellectual nourishment.

In stressing the importance—the indispensability—of disciplinary thinking, I have drawn examples from students in precollegiate or liberal arts education. And indeed, these are the appropriate locales for initial mastery of the ways of thinking of science, mathematics, history, and the arts. I applaud the fact that, in making decisions about admissions, many professional schools give greater weight to success in these disciplinary tracks than they do to prelaw, premed, prebusiness, or preengineering courses of study. After all, the purpose of the professional school is to train you in the particular profession, and the best preparation is one in which one's mind becomes disciplined in the major scholarly ways of thinking.

As one shifts to professional training—whether at a graduate school (as in law or medicine) or a high-level apprenticeship (as happens in many consultancies, book publishing, or journalism)—the disciplinary accent changes. Far less decontextualized learning—far fewer tests based simply on reading and lecture: one is thrown gradually or harshly into a world that more closely resembles the world of practice. We might say that the focus now is on discipline in action. It does not help simply to understand that a lawyer or engineer or manager thinks differently; placed in the shoes of the lawyer, engineer, or manager, one must act differently as well. Thinking and action are more closely allied than ever before. Those who are unable to acquire the distinctive practices, or, in Donald Schön's phrase, to become "reflective practitioners,"[4] should be counseled out of the profession—or, if I may be permitted a wisecrack, should be encouraged to become professors.

Perhaps at one time, an individual could acquire his professional license and then coast on his laurels for the next thirty or even fifty years. I know of no career—from manager to minister—to which this characterization still applies. Indeed, the more important the profession is considered to be, and the higher the position an individual occupies within that profession, the more essential to continue one's education, broadly construed. Sometimes the lifelong learning occurs in formal courses; more often, in informal seminars, executive retreats, high-level conversations and war stories, even in reading books like this one. To some extent, the disciplinary training involves acquisition of new skills—for example, ones connected to technological or financial innovations; but at least as important are new and higher levels of understanding within the disciplines as traditionally constituted. Thus, the scholar comes to understand the various ways in which new knowledge is developed and propagated; the executive comes to understand which managerial capacities are needed for specific niches, which are much more generic, how leadership must adjust to changing conditions in the media or the marketplace. One could attempt to teach these ideas in professional schools, but for the most part they would not be well understood. We might say that these constitute the disciplinary curriculum for later life.

THE OTHER KIND OF DISCIPLINE

That brings us to the other, equally important sense of *discipline*. An individual is disciplined to the extent that she has acquired the habits that allow her to make steady and essentially unending progress in the mastery of a skill, craft, or body of knowledge. With young children, we tend to think of discipline with respect to athletics and the arts. A child disciplined in that sense returns to the basketball or the tennis court each day and practices her moves; or, to shift to the arts, such a child works steadily to improve her violin playing or her calligraphy or her balletic plié. However, an equally important connotation of discipline occurs within a scholastic context. The primary student disciplined in that respect practices her reading or sums or writing each day (OK—she can have alternate Sundays off!); the secondary student works faithfully on her scientific lab exercises, her geometric proofs, or her analysis of written and graphic documents drawn from history. As a child, I practiced on the piano keyboard each afternoon; now with equivalently steady regularity, I revert to the computer keyboard each evening. Whether those forms of disciplines are integrally related remains controversial: despite the wishes of parents, pedagogues, and some psychologists, individuals can be quite disciplined in one sphere and notably erratic in others.

The earliest writers about education stressed the importance of daily drill, study, practice, mastery. Unlike the disciplinary understanding sketched earlier, this kind of discipline has hardly had to fight for a place in the schools. Indeed, it sometimes appears as if observers praise this form for its own sake. Such observers call for more homework even when evidence indicates that it does little or no good in the primary years; they praise the child who sits dutifully at her desk at home and tear their hair out when a child has the television or the CD blaring, or refuses to take out the books until the evening (or the early morning) before the final examination.

In the future, we need a less ritualistic, more deeply internalized form of discipline. Such a disciplined individual continues to learn, but not because she has been programmed to spend two hours a night hitting the books. Rather, she continues to learn, to develop her disciplinary understanding, for two other reasons: (1) she realizes that, given the accumulation of new data, knowledge, and methods, she must become a lifelong student; (2) she has come to enjoy—indeed, she has become passionate about—the process of learning about the world. This motivation should be equally apparent in the executive who ventures to exotic locales and attends institutes, giving up the opportunity to ski, snorkel, or play hooky; and in the physician who regularly surveys several Web sites and journals dedicated to her specialty. As Plato remarked so many years ago, "Through education we need to help students find pleasure in what they have to learn."

DISCIPLINE GONE AWRY

In considering the five minds, for the most part I concentrate on how to nurture each one. Still, it is salutary to remember that every psychological capacity has its pathological form. It is good to be careful, undesirable to be obsessive-compulsive. It is great to experience "flow"—but one should experience that phenomenal state from creative acts that are constructive and not from ones that are criminal, dangerous, or foolish.

With respect to the disciplined mind, a number of cautionary notes should be registered. To begin with, every discipline has its excessive forms: we all joke about the lawyer who brings his legal arguments to the kitchen table, the basketball court, or the bedroom.

Specific disciplines can also come to dominate discourse unduly. Fifty years ago, behavior was seen primarily through a psychoanalytic lens: nowadays, evolutionary psychology and Rational Choice Theory exercise excessive influence in the academy and on the streets. Individuals need to be aware of the limits of the mastered disciplines, when to draw on them, when to temper or shelve them. Having more than one disciplinary skill is an advantage here; one can, for example, consider a work of art from a number of perspectives, ranging from aesthetic to biographical to commercial. Of course, it is important not to confuse those perspectives with one another, or to invoke one when it is manifestly inappropriate in a given context.

Is it possible to be *too* disciplined? As a person of German (and Jewish) background, I am tempted to answer "No," if not "Nein." I do believe that one can become ever more deeply entrenched in a discipline and that even greater depth can be advantageous for one's work. But one wants to avoid two perils. First of all, a discipline should not be pursued obsessively, compulsively, for its own sake. One's understanding of law should deepen because such depth yields understanding and pleasure; simply reading every case that is published and parading one's knowledge thereof is a sign of immaturity, not judgment. And then, too, one must remain ever aware that no topic can be fully mastered from a single disciplinary perspective. One must remain humble about the leverage gained from one discipline, or indeed, even from a multitude of disciplines. Methods should be tools, not chains.

Recently, I have heard of young piano prodigies who play the piano seven, eight, or even more hours a day. Sometimes they are cajoled to do so by overly ambitious parents or teachers; sometimes, remarkably, they want to sustain such a regimen themselves. Over a short period of time, such immersion can be justified, and it may do no harm. But such a slavish routine suggests a lack of distance on what disciplinary immersion can and cannot obtain, and what the long-term costs might be.

One of the greatest pianists ever was Artur Rubinstein (who eventually anglicized his name to Arthur). As a youth, Rubinstein was a prodigy, and, like most prodigies, he worked very hard on his craft. Once he became world renowned—feted wherever he traveled—he ceased to work on his craft with sufficient regularity and assiduity. A frank self-examination elicited a depressing picture:

> *I must confess with sorrow that I was not very proud of myself. The dissipated life I was leading, my constant preoccupation with the opposite sex, the late hours spent nightly with my intellectual friends, the theaters, the shows, the rich food at lunch and dinner, and worst of all, my passionate attraction for all of this never allowed me to concentrate on my work. I prepared my concerts using the large repertoire I had accumulated but without the urge to play better, without referring to the text, relying entirely on my fine memory and my cleverly acquired knowledge of how to use certain encores to arouse the audience to the right pitch of enthusiasm. To put it in a nutshell, I couldn't boast of one single piece which I played entirely faithful to the text and without some technical shortcomings . . . I knew that I was born a true musician but instead of developing my talent I was living on the capital of it.*[5]

Rubinstein came to realize that he could not live on this capital indefinitely without replenishing it. As he commented to an acquaintance, "When I don't practice for a day, I know. When I don't practice for two days, the orchestra knows it. And when I don't practice for three days, the world knows it."[6] And so he gradually relinquished the life of the sybarite, settled down, launched a family, and began to practice the repertoire with greater regularity and scrupulousness. Unlike most pianists, he was able to play publicly and at a high level throughout his seventies and eighties. He stands as an example of someone who was ultimately able to wed the two meanings of discipline: mastery of a craft, and the capacity to renew that craft through regular application over the years.

I hope to have convinced you that, while the process is arduous, a disciplined mind can be fashioned; and that its achievement represents an important, indeed indispensable, milestone. Alas, a disciplined mind alone no longer suffices. More and more knowledge now lies in the spaces between, or the connections across, the several disciplines. In the future, individuals must learn how to synthesize knowledge and how to extend it in new and unfamiliar ways.

CHAPTER **3**

The Synthesizing Mind

"Hell is a place where nothing connects with nothing."

—VARTAN GREGORIAN, CITING DANTE

IN THE WESTERN sacred tradition, the story of human beings begins in the Garden of Eden, when Adam was enticed to take a first bite of fruit from the Tree of Knowledge. For the generations that immediately followed the biblical Adam, knowledge accumulated at a sufficiently slow rate that it could be passed on orally (though perhaps not in apple-sized chunks), from parent to child, and on down to each succeeding generation. But humans are distinguished by the fact that we continue to accumulate knowledge at increasingly rapid rates. Indeed, the Bible itself represents an effort to collate the most important knowledge that had accrued to that point—knowledge heavily skewed, of course, toward religious and moral messages.

Once societies became self-conscious about the knowledge that had coalesced, an occurrence that may have been yoked to the advent of literacy, groups attempted to set down what was known in ways that were clear, systematic, and easily grasped by the next generation. In the Western secular tradition, the pre-Socratic philosophers were the first individuals who sought to order current knowledge. Their successors—Socrates, Plato, and, most especially, Aristotle—strove to collate not only knowledge of how to live but also, perhaps especially, the extant knowledge about the world as it was understood at that time. The books of Aristotle—*Physics, Metaphysics, Poetics, Rhetoric*, among many others—represent the curriculum that had been delineated. No wonder that Aristotle was known for nearly two millennia as The Philosopher. Yet Aristotle was not alone. A formidable line of synthesizers exists in the West, from Aristotle to St. Augustine to St. Thomas Aquinas (in many ways Aristotle's Christian counterpart); and then on to the literary Dante, the prodigiously talented Leonardo, the encyclopedists of the eighteenth century, the *Encyclopedia Britannica*'s micropedia and macropedia of the late twentieth century, and—most recently—the Wikipedia of the twenty-first century. Similar lineages could be traced out in other major cultural traditions.

The ability to knit together information from disparate sources into a coherent whole is vital today. The amount of accumulated knowledge is reportedly doubling every two or three years (wisdom presumably accrues more slowly!). Sources of information are vast and disparate, and individuals crave coherence and integration. Nobel Prize–winning physicist Murray Gell-Mann has asserted that the mind most at a premium in the twenty-first century will be the mind that can synthesize well.

When I wrote about synthesis in the *Harvard Business Review*, I received an evocative confirmation from Richard Severs, a navy captain: "I have been through this wringer. Synthesizing massive amounts of data, intelligence, slants, opinions, tactics, and trying to maintain a strategic big picture was a challenge. You feel it creeping up into your brain like a numbing cold and you just have to choke it down, sift faster, and stay with it. [It's] challenging to be sure, but if you practice it, you develop a good tool for the leadership toolbox."[1]

Yet the forces that stand in the way of synthesis are formidable. In the previous chapter, I argued that it is difficult for most of us even to think systematically within one scholarly discipline or profession—how much more of a burden to master a number of perspectives and then piece them together in a useful amalgam! Adding to this difficulty is the fact that individual cognition is remarkably domain-specific: as a species, we are predisposed to learn skills in certain contexts and to resist—or at least find challenging—their wider generalization and broader application. Few individuals and even fewer institutions have expertise in inculcating the skill of synthesis. And, just to top it off, even when synthesizing is desired and cultivated, we lack standards for determining when a productive synthesis has been accomplished, as opposed to when the proposed synthesis is premature, misguided, or even fundamentally wrongheaded. As turns out to be the case with each of the other minds portrayed here, the mind-that-would-synthesize must grapple with forces that seem to be arrayed against its proper realization.

KINDS OF SYNTHESIS

Against the odds, individuals seek synthesis. Successful examples can be cited. Such syntheses require us to put together elements that were originally discrete or disparate.

Here are the most common kinds, along with some impressive illustrations:

1. *Narratives.* The synthesizer puts material together into a coherent narrative. Examples range from the Bible to a contemporary history or social science textbook. Narratives

exist no less in fiction (Tolstoy's *War and Peace*) than in the nonfictional realm (Gibbon's *Decline and Fall of the Roman Empire*).

2. *Taxonomies.* Materials are ordered in terms of salient characteristics. Consider the Dewey decimal system in the library, the Linnaean classification of plants and animals, a double-entry balance sheet in an annual report. Such taxonomies are often presented in charts or tables. The Russian Mendeleyev succeeded where the alchemists of earlier eras had failed: he was able to produce an ordered periodic table of the elements of the earth. And because he understood the principles that gave rise to their detailed atomic structure, this synthesizing scientist was even able to predict the existence of elements that had not yet been discovered.

3. *Complex concepts.* A newly stipulated concept can tie together or blend a range of phenomena. Charles Darwin achieved such a synthesis in his concept of natural selection; Sigmund Freud developed the concept of the unconscious; Adam Smith introduced the concept of the division of labor. In literary analysis, T. S. Eliot created the concept of the *objective correlative*—the embodiment of an emotion in a particular situation, such that the reader will infer the intended emotion without its being explicitly mentioned. In business, Michael Porter construed strategy as a synthesis of five forces that together determine potential profit. And note the plethora of concepts in financial analysis: the business cycle, price-earnings ratio, the eighty-twenty principle (also known as Pareto's law).

4. *Rules and aphorisms.* Much of folk wisdom is captured and conveyed by short phrases, designed to be memorable and widely applicable. Across societies, nearly everyone learns some version of the phrases "Think first, act second,"

"Don't try to juggle too many balls at the same time," "An ounce of prevention is worth a pound of cure." Such different truths also permeate the workplace. "Great cases make bad law," lawyers are taught. "Diversify your portfolio" is the watchword among investors. Corporate executives favor succinct mission statements, like IBM's "Think" or GE's "Progress is our most important product." And scientists are counseled, "Always replicate an experiment; and the more surprising the result, the greater the imperative to replicate."

5. *Powerful metaphors, images, and themes.* Individuals may bring concepts to life by invoking metaphors. Darwin described evolution as a branching tree and speciation as a tangled bank; Freud saw the unconscious as the region underneath conscious thought, and the id as the horse that could jerk around the ego-rider; Adam Smith characterized the self-regulatory nature of markets through the image of the invisible hand. Metaphors may be presented graphically as well as verbally. Historian of science Gerald Holton points out that synthesizers often base their key ideas on underlying "themata" of which they themselves may not be consciously aware.[2] For example, both Freud and Darwin saw life as a struggle between deadly opposing forces, while Smith envisioned a harmonious society, based on principles of exchange. Corporations create brands—in words, graphics, and jingles.

6. *Embodiments without words.* So far, my examples have been drawn primarily from academic subjects and from daily life. Powerful syntheses can also be embodied in works of art. Consider Picasso's famed *Guernica*, in which the violent forces of the Spanish Civil War are captured in a single cubist-style mural; Hogarth's evocative *Rake's Progress*,

which chronicles the pathetic dissolution of a libertine; and perhaps the most famous synthesis of all, Michelangelo's illustrations of biblical events on the ceiling of the Sistine Chapel. Syntheses exist as well in other arts: Wagner's *Ring Cycle*, Gaudi's unfinished Sagrada Familia Cathedral in Barcelona, Stravinsky's ballet *Le sacre du printemps*, Martha Graham's modernist re-creations of southwestern Native American rituals, Charlie Chaplin's *Modern Times*, and Ingmar Bergman's *Wild Strawberries* spring to mind.

7. *Theories.* Concepts can be amalgamated into a theory. Darwin's theory of evolution combines the concepts of variation, competition, natural selection, and survival until reproduction; Freud's psychoanalytic theory is built on the concepts of repression, infantile sexuality, free association, and the unconscious. Adam Smith's theory of a market economy weaves together ideas of supply and demand, labor, production, profit, and loss.

8. *Metatheory.* It is possible to propose an overall framework for knowledge, as well as a "theory of theories." Georg Wilhelm Friedrich Hegel portrayed an inexorable universal developmental sequence—hence the "meta"—from thesis to antithesis to synthesis; flipping Hegel on his head, Karl Marx viewed economic/material factors as determinant, with ideas emerging as a superstructure. Thomas Kuhn argued that new scientific paradigms are by definition incommensurate with their predecessors: proponents of the new paradigm must wait until the advocates of the once entrenched paradigm have passed from the scene. Philosopher of knowledge Jean-François Lyotard questions the legitimacy of such overarching theories—with the exception of the metatheory that there are no proper metatheories!

COMPONENTS OF SYNTHESIS

So much for the kinds of mental feats that can be termed "syntheses." The achievement of an effective synthesis—even one far less grand than the famous ones just mentioned—is a considerable feat. At a minimum, any effort to synthesize entails four loosely ordered components:

1. *A goal—a statement or conception of what the synthesizer is trying to achieve.* Examples range from Freud's desire to create a psychology of the mind to Picasso's aim of capturing on canvas the destruction of an entire town.

2. *A starting point—an idea, image, or, indeed, any previous work on which to build.* Darwin began his efforts using earlier evolutionary theories, on the one hand, and his observations on the *Beagle*, on the other. Eliot's *Waste Land* drew on his own earlier poetic renderings of desolation and on many, often obscure, texts in a variety of languages and idioms.

3. *Selection of strategy, method, and approach.* Here is where the synthesizer's disciplinary training comes into play. The synthesizer must choose the format of his ultimate synthesis— for example, one of the eight kinds that I just introduced. Then drawing on tools of his discipline, he must proceed, with predictable fits and starts, toward his goal.

   These tools can range from the logical analysis of the philosopher, to the interpretation of texts by literary critics, to the execution of pilot studies by the biologist, to the maintenance of notebooks, sketchpads, and diaries by the draftsperson or the novelist. In developing a business plan, an executive may consult experts, commission studies, run focus groups of managers or customers. There is no guarantor, of course, that the traditional skills of the trade will prove adequate or even appropriate for the proposed synthesis. And

so the choice of tool must always be tentative, subject to re-
vision or even, on occasion, to wholesale rejection.

4. *Drafts and feedback.* Sooner or later, the synthesizer must
take an initial crack at a synthesis: the abstract of the paper,
the outline of the lecture or chapter, the model for the
building or statue, the beta business plan. This first stab can
even be a provisional synthesis in itself. We know from the
notebooks of master creators—Picasso, Freud, Darwin,
Martha Graham—that first drafts are often primitive and
yet may contain the crucial nucleus of the final version.
Philosopher Charles Sanders Peirce claimed that these
preternaturally shrewd guesses involved a special mental
power that he termed "abduction."

To ground this discussion, consider the situation of the newly re-
cruited turnaround executive who announces a concrete goal: a review of what has gone wrong in recent years and a concrete plan for
correcting course. That will be her exercise of synthesis. Of course, the
executive is well advised to do a lot of listening, watching, studying, and
conferring—and to avoid badmouthing her predecessors and her new
colleagues. Still, she needs a starting point—the best understanding
available of what has happened in the company and the viable options.
That, indeed, would *be* her default synthesis had she no time or resources whatsoever. The precious months allow her to devise a strategy
for reviewing records, accumulating information from present and past
employees and informed observers; testing out various options and
scenarios; coming to understand the company, its past, and its current
competitive landscape. At a certain point, however, she must stop the
input and the reflection and turn her attention to the preparation of
the best synthesis that she can muster. If she is fortunate, she will have
time for feedback and a number of additional iterations. More often
than not, however, the clock will be ticking with increasing impa-
tience and she will have to "satisfice" with her second or third draft.

Of the eight formats outlined, what form is the executive likely to use? The most common form of synthesis is the narrative—a form accessible to almost everyone. Powerful images and metaphors are always welcome. Within the narrative form, the executive is free to use aphorisms, concepts, and taxonomies. To the extent that she can embody her synthesis in her own behavior, that is all to the good. But unless she is dealing with a sophisticated audience (or trying to get tenure at a university), she should steer clear of theories. We need not worry that she will be tempted to produce a metatheory!

With respect to the executive, let me be clear: by no means does her task end when a synthesis has been fashioned. The synthesis is but a first step in turning the company around. At least as important is the development of a strategy, the execution of that strategy, the inevitable correcting of one's course along the way. Indeed, while it may be optional for the rest of us, a strategic mind is a necessity for an executive But the strategy of the executive is far more likely to be effective if it is based on a solid, thoroughly vetted synthesis.

INTERDISCIPLINARY SYNTHESES: THE REWARDS, THE RISKS

Perhaps the most ambitious form of synthesis occurs in *interdisciplinary work*. This phrase should not be invoked lightly. We would not consider an individual to be bilingual unless he or she had mastered more than one language. By the same token, it is inappropriate to characterize work as genuinely interdisciplinary unless it entails the proper combination of at least two disciplines. Moreover, at least in the ideal, the two disciplines should not merely be juxtaposed; they should be genuinely integrated. Such an integration should yield understanding that could not have been achieved solely within either of the parent disciplines.

The term *interdisciplinary* is much bandied about these days. It is worth differentiating two distinct forms. Within the academy, as I've just noted, the term *interdisciplinary* is applied to studies that draw deliberately on at least two scholarly disciplines and seek a synergistic integration. Biochemists combine biological and chemical knowledge; historians of science apply the tools of history to one or more fields of science. In professional life, interdisciplinary is typically applied to a team composed of workers who have different professional training. In a medical setting, an interdisciplinary team might consist of one or more surgeons, anesthesiologists, radiologists, nurses, therapists, and social workers. In a business setting, an interdisciplinary or cross-functional team might feature inventors, designers, marketers, the sales force, and representatives drawn from different levels of management. The cutting-edge interdisciplinary team is sometimes dubbed Skunk Works: members are granted considerable latitude on the assumption that they will exit their habitual silos and engage in the boldest forms of connection making.

Each form of synthesis can be done more or less well. Narratives can be incoherent, jerky, or forced—consider an American history text that ignored Native Americans or perseverated on the Puritan heritage. Taxonomies can be premature or illegitimate—consider the many fruitless efforts to array various metals on the part of gold-seeking alchemists over the centuries. Concepts can be misleading—for example, the psychologist's notion of intelligence ignores artistic and social manifestations of intellect. Metaphors can be deceptive—the domino theory of nations falling one-by-one to communism turned out to be wrong. Theories often fall in the face of uncomfortable facts: communism was "the god that failed," and, counter to Marx's predictions, has survived in the least developed, rather than the most developed, countries. Adam Smith's laissez-faire economics has to be "repaired" through Keynesian interventions on the part of the government. And as I've noted earlier,

French philosopher Jean-François Lyotard deems the quest for metatheories to be doomed.

The dangers of inadequate synthesis are perhaps most manifest when it comes to interdisciplinary work. To begin with, much activity in the early years of schooling is misleadingly labeled as "interdisciplinary." Children may well benefit from carrying out evocative classroom projects or from pursuing a unit on generative topics like "patterns" or "water" or the "cradle of civilization." But these endeavors do not involve disciplines in any legitimate sense of that term. In making a diorama or a dance, in thinking of water or cities in a variety of ways, students are drawing on common sense, common experiences, or common terminology and examples. If no single discipline is being applied, then clearly interdisciplinary thinking cannot be at work.

Even when students have begun to master the disciplines singularly, there is no guarantee that a combination of disciplines will be appropriately or productively linked. Courses may well and appropriately involve both history and the arts. One can read about the battles of the Spanish Civil War in a history text *and* one can also look at the painting *Guernica*, or read the novels of André Malraux or Ernest Hemingway, without making any particular effort to link or compare these sources. We might term this approach "disciplinary juxtaposition"—a failure to realize the illumination that may accrue when different perspectives are synergistically joined.

Even when genuine efforts are made to link the disciplines, there is no guarantee that the link will be well motivated or freshly illuminating. If, for example, an individual takes artistic depiction too literally and assumes that the novelist Malraux is a reporter, or that the cubist Picasso is a realistic painter, inappropriate inferences will be drawn. Evolutionary psychology makes a lot of sense when it attempts to explain the different behavioral patterns displayed by males and females in courtship or sexual congress; evolutionary psychology strays when it seeks to explicate historical trends or artistic tastes.

Analogous perils can be observed in the professional and business spheres. Take journalism. Reporters, editors, publishers, members of the audience, and shareholders may all be involved in the same broadcast or print outlet; but there is no guarantee that representatives drawn from these different populations will see things in the same way or that they will be able to work together smoothly. Multinational corporations like 3M, BP, or Sony all employ scientists, human resource personnel, accountants, marketers, and IT specialists; but one can expect problems in communication when these disparate experts are all thrown together on a task force and asked to come up with a design for a new recreation center.

Don't get me wrong. Interdisciplinary investigation is very important, and the best interdisciplinary work is at a distinct premium in our era. Our studies suggest that such work is typically motivated by one of three considerations:

1. *A powerful new concept has been developed, and it is inviting and timely to test the reach of that concept.* For example, in recent years, mathematicians have developed theories of complexity, chaos, and catastrophes. These theories turn out to have important applications—both explanatory and methodological—in the physical sciences. But it is legitimate to question whether instructive instances of complexity can be discerned within other sciences (e.g., biology), social sciences (e.g., economics), and perhaps even in the humanities (e.g., political history, art history).

   A parallel instance exists in the business world—the idea of inexpensive disruptive technologies that aid newcomers while threatening to displace the older, larger, and more complacent players in a sector.[3] It is useful for individuals across the business and professional worlds to become acquainted with this concept. It remains an open question to what extent the concept of disruptive technologies applies to different sectors, to different niches within a sector, and to nonprofit entities like universities or nongovernmental organizations.[4] Moreover, what counts as disruptive in the technological sphere might be quite different from what is actually disruptive in the areas of sales or human resources.

2. *An important phenomenon has emerged, and a full understanding of that phenomenon calls for, or even demands, its contextualization.* In most cases one begins to understand the theory of relativity in terms of constituent concepts from physics and mathematics. A broader and more nuanced understanding of relativity may emerge as one acquires familiarity with the history of science in the late nineteenth century; events occurring in other domains, including challenges to orthodoxy in politics and in the arts; and the particular issues with which Einstein was wrestling, ranging from his reading of classics in the philosophy of science to his daily assignments as a patent officer, which included efforts to ascertain the precise moment when a train was arriving at a distant destination.[5]

A quite different example emerges from the medical sphere. Tests of genetic screening allow an unambiguous determination of who will be struck by a disease like Huntington's chorea and a probabilistic determination of who is likely to contract various cancers. The question of whether to share this information with potential victims and their families, and, if so, how best to share that information, is not one that can be left alone to the geneticist or even to the family physician or minister. Ideally, teams composed of geneticists, genetic therapists, physicians, social workers, religious leaders, and ethicists should weigh in on this decision: and yet, there is no guarantee that individuals with different disciplinary training will—or even should—conceptualize this vexing issue in the same way.

Nor is this example remote from corporate life. Suppose a widely heralded new drug turns out to produce toxic side effects in a very small proportion of the population. Alas, the historical record documents a strong tendency on the part of executives to attempt to hide or sugarcoat this finding. But even in those cases where there is consensus to come clean, strong disagreements may persist among experts concerning the way in which the announcement is made, the manner in which physicians and patients are informed, the preparations surrounding the public announcement, and subsequent changes to be made (or not made) in the company's research, launching, and withdrawal of new drugs.

3. *A pressing problem emerges, and current individual disciplines prove inadequate to solve that problem.* Newspapers are filled with reports on troubling conditions—widespread poverty, the spread of fatal diseases, the pollution of the environment, threats to privacy, the ever looming specter of terrorism—that cry out for solution. Such challenges cannot even be understood, let alone addressed, unless several disciplines and professions can be brought to bear. And so, even when the researcher or policymaker would *prefer* to work within the confines of a single discipline, it soon becomes evident that one needs to call on other disciplines—for example, virology, demography, immunology, behavioral psychology, and social network theory in the case of the spread and treatment of AIDS.

Note that none of these synthesizing efforts arises in a vacuum. In each case, there is a motivating goal; an initial stance taken by the synthesizer; a set of tools or strategies that can be employed; one or more interim syntheses; and at least some criteria by which the success of the synthesis can be evaluated. And to repeat: the synthesis is not the same as a successfully executed strategy, but it may well be the essential point of departure.

PROMISING AND OVERPROMISING SYNTHESES

Syntheses are put forth all the time—for example, most textbooks and many trade books (including this one!) are frank efforts to synthesize knowledge about a possibly unwieldy topic so that it can be assimilated by a target audience. Determining what constitutes an adequate synthesis in abstract terms is not possible; as with the proverbial question "Does a string stretch across a room?" the answer must be contextualized. It turns out that arriving at an adequate synthesis is challenging, and anticipating the criteria for a judgment even more so.

As it happens, two books with similar-sounding titles offer me a chance to tackle these conundrums. In 2003, travel writer Bill Bryson published a book with the grand title *A Short History of Nearly Everything*. In about five hundred pages of richly documented text, Bryson attempts to summarize and illustrate what science has discovered about the physical and human worlds. As he charmingly puts it: "For you to be here now, trillions of drifting atoms had somehow to assemble in an intricate and intriguingly obliging manner to create you. It's an arrangement so specialized and particular that it has never been tried before and will only exist this once."[6]

Bryson begins with discoveries about the cosmos, discussing what we know about the universe, how it began, its various celestial bodies, and our place within that firmament; moves on to geological knowledge about the planet earth, covering its size, its age, and its constituent elements, including the tiniest quantum particles; and then surveys findings about human biology, ranging from the origins of life on the planet to its current efflorescence, from single-cell organisms to the most complex of primates, and from our own origins as single cells to the ten thousand trillion cells that constitute the adult human body. He concludes with the amusing notion that Isaac Newton's monumental *Principia* appeared at about the time that the dodo bird became extinct. As he puts it: "[Y]ou would be hard pressed, I would submit, to find a better pairing of occurrences to illustrate the divine and felonious nature of the human being—a species of organisms that is capable of unpacking the deepest secrets of the heavens while at the same time pounding into extinction, for no purpose at all, a creature that never did us any harm and wasn't even remotely capable of understanding what we were doing to it as we did it."[7]

Bryson's synthesis works for me. He covers a huge amount of ground but in a way that makes logical sense, and constitutes a good story to boot. Rather than dropping a thousand names or a thousand facts, he presents a handful of fascinating, specific stories in detail, draws the appropriate lessons, and discerns links between them. Always, the big picture of the enormous and the infinitesimal, the remote and the intimate, remains at the forefront. And he never loses sight of himself as the well-meaning but hardly omniscient guide, and us, the readers, as the scientifically half-educated, but eager-to-learn audience. That may be because, according to his own testimony, Bryson was not an expert when he began research for this book. Rather (recalling Dante being chaperoned by Virgil), he was the learner, who wanted to understand enough so that he could share his own synthesis with a new cohort of readers. In my view the gentle teacher succeeds.

I am less buoyed by Ken Wilber's *A Brief History of Everything*. Wilber is widely recognized as an intellectual polymath—a largely self-educated scholar who has mastered vast bodies of knowledge in philosophy, theology, science, and psychology (among many other disciplines) and who strives relentlessly to put them together into one overarching theoretical framework. To the best of my knowledge, he is by far the most ambitious synthesizer at work in the English language and by many yardsticks the most successful.

In various works, including the aforementioned book, Wilber attempts to order all of our knowledge into taxonomies, grids, hierarchies. The frames that he uses include going from the physical to the psychological, from the lowest forms of cognition to the highest planes of consciousness; locating all disciplines in terms of their contributions to his holistic view; grouping together dozens of theorists into an overarching frame; and, above all, trying to relate all of these dimensions to the highest realm, the realm of the spiritual—"where Spirit becomes conscious of itself, awakens to itself, begins to recognize its own true nature."[8] By "the spiritual," Wilber is not referring to a particular religion; indeed, as his admirers insist, he has bridged the Eastern and Western concepts of the spirit. Wilber believes he has discerned a remarkable consensus among thinkers the world over, "whether living today or six thousand years ago, whether from New Mexico in the Far West or from Japan in the Far East."[9]

To convey the somewhat problematic nature of the Wilberian enterprise, it is best to give a few examples from his own writings. Asked about the relation between depth and consciousness, he says, "Consciousness is simply what depth looks like from the inside, from within. So, yes, depth is everywhere, consciousness is everywhere, Spirit is everywhere. And as depth increases, consciousness increasingly awakens, Spirit increasingly unfolds. To say that evolution produces greater depth is simply to say that it unfolds greater consciousness."[10] Explicating his procedure, he reports:

I simply started making lists of all of these holarchical maps—conventional and new age, premodern and modern and postmodern—everything from systems theory to the Great Chain of Being, from the Buddhist vijanas to Piaget, Marx, Kohlberg, the Vedantic koshas, Loevinger, Maslow, Lenski, Kabbalah and so on. I had literally hundreds of these things, these maps, spread out on legal pads all over the floor . . . I thought that I might be able to find the single and basic holarchy that they were all trying to represent in their own ways . . . [I]t was very obvious that each holarchy in each group

*was indeed dealing with the same territory but overall we had four
different territories so to speak.*[11]

Without doubt, this is a noble effort; if Wilber did not attempt
it, others surely would. Why, then, am I ungratified, unsatisfied? I
think it is because Wilber emerges as the ultimate "lumper." He is
always poised to see connections; to join theories, stories, examples
together; to accentuate their commonalities; to pinpoint their order
in a yet greater order. An example of his compulsion to lump
comes from this quotation: "In recent times, cultural evolution has
been championed, in various ways, by Jürgen Habermas, Gerald
Heard, Michael Murphy, W. G. Runciman, Sisirkumar Ghose, Alas-
tair Taylor, Gerhard Lenski, Jean Houston, Duane Elgin, Jay Earley,
Daniel Dennett, Robert Bellah, Erwin Laszlo, Kishore Gandhi, and
Jean Gebser, to name a few."[12] Far from being an isolated example,
statements of this sort appear dozens if not hundreds of times in his
voluminous writings.

"Lumpers" are contrasted with "splitters." Splitters make distinctions, enjoy contrasts, always ask, "Why do these *not* connect?
What is the difference, what is the *crucial* distinction?" On a continuum of lumpers to splitters, I fall somewhere in the middle. Yet,
confronted by one of Wilber's texts, I feel myself strangely antagonistic to lumping. When everything connects to everything else—
in, what Wilber likes to term the Great Chain of Being—then one
is hard pressed to make priorities, distinctions, illuminating comparisons. It would be difficult to know how to disprove Wilber, indeed, where to start, where to discern the tensions and struggles
that permeate Bryson's text but which are inevitably papered over
in Wilber's compulsive search for connective tissue. His effort virtually paralyzes the critical mind.

I admit that my preference of Bryson over Wilber is a matter of
taste. And I remain grateful to Wilber for opening my eyes to many
literatures and to making a place for my own writings in his own
vast scheme. For those committed to lumping, Wilber is a prophet.

I fear, however, that his syntheses will make sense only for those who already buy his major premise—his organizing themata—that all can be organized into one giant scheme. It is unlikely to win converts among the skeptical, to gain allegiance among the splitters.

WHY SYNTHESIS IS DIFFICULT BUT POSSIBLE

The mind of the young person is characterized by two powerful but contradictory features. On the one hand, preschool children readily discern connections—indeed, they are forever drawing comparisons. A banana is treated as a cell phone (though rarely is the reverse observed—at least, to this point in cultural history!); a stick doubles as a hobbyhorse; parallel lines on the road are called "zebra stripes"; the past tense of *swim* is assumed to be *swimmed*. Comparisons extend beyond single objects or actions. Listening to a march by John Philip Sousa, a five-year-old may compare it to a train ride; introduced to the concept of separation of powers in the U.S. government, the ten-year-old may envision it as a three-pronged seesaw, with each prong in the ascendancy for a time until a balance has been restored.

Given this proclivity to connect, it is not surprising that young persons attempt to integrate or synthesize. The problem, of course, is that many such connections prove to be superficial or even fundamentally wrong-headed. The term *relativity* has been applied both to Picasso's cubism and to Einstein's physics, but neither phenomenon is illuminated by this superficial coupling. *Swimmed* may generalize a rule, but it is not an acceptable past tense. Seesaws (at least the two-legged versions) may tend toward equilibrium, but branches of government can clash or be overpowered. Absent the relevant disciplines, and a metric for judging appropriateness, the human "connecting" proclivity is charming but hardly sufficient. (Ken Wilber might well disagree!)

By the time of middle childhood, the human connecting impulse has been chastened or corralled. Studies of metaphoric capacity indicate that preschool children are more likely than their older counterparts to produce metaphors—charming ones as well as inappropriate ones. Youngsters age six and above exercise a blue pencil. Searching for the appropriate connection or characterization, they revert to literal similarities, while avoiding ones that may entail inexact or illegitimate connections. To be sure, the capacity for appreciating comparisons remains; and yet, with age, most individuals shy away from proposing fresh comparisons. Only poets seem inoculated against the attenuation of metaphor-making proclivities.

An even more powerful force militates against integration. As I've already noted several times, human beings turn out to be creatures that are quite context- or site-specific. We acquire actions, behaviors, thoughts, skills in one situation, and we may master these. However, as we grow older, most of us become conservative (I note exceptions in the next chapter on creative minds). We maintain those features in the settings in which they have been learned, and perhaps we stretch them a bit. But we are loath to apply skills or concepts widely, let alone promiscuously. Speaking more generally, the mind is organized not as an all-purpose computer; it is more precisely conceptualized as a set of relatively independent modules. Just how or when or why these modules should ever connect remains obscure to many theorists of psychology.

This conservatism may be helpful—or at least neutral—to the teacher of individual disciplines. However, it poses a heavy burden on those who would foster interdisciplinary thought or the effecting of powerful syntheses, let alone original creations. In their English classes, young persons may learn how to write effective prose; but if they fail to transport at least part of those lessons across the hallway to history class or to biology lab assignments, then they have missed an opportunity to link compositional strategies. Adolescents may be exposed to causal reasoning in their physics classes;

but if they draw no lessons about argumentation in history or geometry class, then this form of thinking needs to be retaught. Adults at Corporation A may interact comfortably with those on their team and yet clash sharply with team members from Corporation B, with which their organization has recently merged. It is useful to keep in mind that, as a species, we evolved to survive in distinctive ecological niches; we did not evolve in order to have correct theories, to master disciplines, or to transfer lessons encountered in one setting appropriately to others. The young child overgeneralizes; the older child prefers to resist generalizations even when they may be apt.

Professional training only reinforces these tendencies. As the journalist learns to convey the essence of a story to a lay reader in 150 words, her ability to craft lengthier reports, or to speak to highly trained experts, may wane. Asked to collaborate on a book with a working scientist or historian, the journalist may become quite frustrated. As the physician learns to diagnose disease from reading computer printouts, and as she witnesses dozens of deaths in the emergency room, she may become insensitive to individual human suffering. Teamed up on a complex case with a minister or social worker, the physician may have difficulty in communicating with these experts and may strike family members as being remote. The veteran engineer who hits a home run when asked to find a snag in the electronic circuitry may strike out when required to resolve a conflict or manage a division.

Individuals differ significantly in their predisposition to metaphorize, and in their capacity or inclination to transfer lessons from one class or discipline to another. Aristotle deemed the capacity to create apt metaphors as a sign of genius. The anthropologist Claude Lévi-Strauss contrasts the *bricoleur*—the handyman who tackles a problem by fitting together whatever bric-a-brac happens to be lying around—with the scientist, whose preferred approach is deductive. In my own work, I have distinguished between two intellectual approaches. *Laser intelligence* probes deeply into a topic but ignores opportunities to cross-pollinate; it's perhaps best suited for disciplinary work. *Searchlight intelligence* may not probe as deeply but is always scanning the environment and may therefore more readily discern connections (and identify differences) across spheres. Both types may synthesize, but the contents that they synthesize and the criteria for success will differ.

The novelist C. P. Snow has written evocatively about these contrasting approaches. Surveying the sciences in the 1920s, he identified biology as an area where a wide, synthesizing mentality was appropriate. At a premium were individuals who were able to take into account findings in many spheres and weave them together in a convincing tapestry. But, says Snow, as expertise accumulates, and as a science takes a mathematical turn, the period for broad synthesis comes to an end. As he laments: "[I]n any science less complete than physics, the more general mind still has its uses, though every day the chances grow less."[13] A premium is placed on individuals who can probe deeper and deeper into a narrow area of scholarship and come up with definitive answers, or decisive refutations. As expertise accrues, the laser replaces the searchlight.

I've observed that two very different kinds of individuals are drawn to interdisciplinary work: those who are curious, well informed, and prone to make well-motivated leaps; and those who spurn orderly linear thinking and are attracted to leaps that may be wild or sloppy. This distinction may be observed at the workplace as well as the classroom. Some executives are gifted with the capacity to take in huge amounts of information but then, in John Gardner's felicitous phrase, are able to "unclutter their minds" and focus on what is truly important.[14] Others leap from one half-baked idea to another, never disciplining their thought, and leaving their employees and outside observers increasingly confused.

One might even speculate that various forms of intelligence gravitate toward different forms of synthesis. With reference to the kinds of synthesis mentioned earlier, perhaps the linguistic mind favors a story; the logical mind, some kind of equation or theory; the spatial mind, a chart or architectonic scheme; the bodily kinesthetic mind, some kind of balance between opposing forces. Should this be the case, the question then arises about whether it is possible to effect a master synthesis among differently shaped integrations—perhaps through one's self-knowledge (in my terms, through the exercise of intrapersonal intelligence). If our hypothetical turn-around executive could achieve such a "synthesis of syntheses," she would be fortunate indeed.

THE EDUCATIONAL CHALLENGE

Can one develop a disciplined mind while at the same time keeping alive the potential for synthetic thinking? In truth, the amount of systematic knowledge about how to inculcate a synthesizing mind—as it were, a "synthesis on synthesizing"—is modest at best. Indeed, if someone were to say, "The best thing is to expose young people to individuals of a synthetic bend, to invite young persons to participate in synthesizing efforts, and to give them regular, useful feedback," I might have to concede that this approach is as likely to succeed as any other.

Still, we should be able to proceed beyond this "toss would-be synthesizers into the bath" advice. Indeed, at each developmental stage, certain experiences and tasks may help induce synthetic thinking. I've already noted the strong, indeed ineluctable, tendency of young children to see, make, and even force connections. This cognitive "polymorphous perversity," if you will, constitutes an invaluable deposit in one's intellectual bank, an investment that can be redeemed at many times and in many ways in the future. Diverse neural networks are being joined; and even if those connections go underground for a while, there is every reason to believe that they endure and can be drawn on in future years. Celebrate, don't censor or curtail, the connections that are effortlessly effected by the young mind.

Alas, under ordinary circumstances, the synthesizing mind achieves little formal attention during the school years. At first the task of acquiring the basic literacies takes center stage; thereafter, the acquisition of disciplinary, or at least subject matter knowledge, becomes the order of the day. Probably the chief "synthesizing nourishment" absorbed by the mind of the nine-year-old, or the fourteen-year-old, comes from the occasional adult synthesizer who is encountered—or from school or mass media presentations that have an integrating flavor. Wide, though admittedly *undisciplined*, reading of books or surfing of the Web may also prove productive in the long run.

I've already noted the role in schools of projects and theme-related curricula. These are well-intentioned efforts to sustain or buoy the potential for making connections. The problem with these pedagogical interventions is readily stated. In most cases educators fail to invoke explicit standards in judging *which* connections, *which* integrations, *which* syntheses are valid, and in which ways they are (or are not) meritorious. To judge a project, one must invoke criteria that come from the appropriate domain—what makes a good essay, a striking mural, a compelling narrative, an effective trademark, a viable business plan—as well as criteria that suit the subject(s) of the project: is this an accurate description of the rain forest, a proper use of the term *rhythm*, a culturally nuanced portrait of a Chinese or Chilean home?

An explicit identification of the constituents of a good project or a viable solution to a problem provides a useful starting point. Models (both successful and not) are essential here. Only if an educator can identify the dimensions that characterize excellent, adequate, and unacceptable projects or solutions is it reasonable to expect students to advance and to begin to engage in timely self-evaluation.

Explicit instruction about forms of synthesis, such as those introduced at the beginning of this chapter, may also be pertinent. Some students, professionals, or executives may arrive on their own at felicitous metaphors or taxonomies or concepts; but many others will benefit from hints about how to create a useful taxonomy, a powerful metaphor, an enlightening concept, a cogent theory. Powerful syntheses involve blends among scripts, frames, concepts that are usually considered separately; as has been demonstrated with respect to mathematical problem solving, there is an art to creating powerful blends or amalgams. Those individuals who can generate several representations of the same idea or concept are far more likely to come up with potent syntheses than those who are limited to a single, often attenuated representation of that idea. Nowadays, instruction along these lines often takes place under the label of "metaknowledge"—coming to understand the building blocks of knowledge in an explicit way. Alluding to this relatively new enterprise, my colleague David Perkins speaks persuasively of the "knowledge arts."

Of special value are useful and supportive critiques of the synthesis, connection, or integration put forth by the student. During the middle years of childhood, educators must keep open the possibilities of connection making and honor the plurality of appropriate connections; at the same time, educators must also identify those syntheses that are lacking or flawed in one or another dimension. With respect to nearly any problem or project, there are responses that are more or less adequate. Students benefit from exposure to different solutions, different methods of arriving at solutions, and different rubrics for evaluation of those solutions. These interventions are by no means restricted to schoolchildren. One reason that I compared Bryson's and Wilber's "brief histories" was to suggest a set of criteria on which putative syntheses might be judged.

Finally, aspiring synthesizers benefit from explicit instruction on strategies. When persons have had some experience in synthesizing, they should be able to step back and identify the major components:

a specific goal or mission; the stance that the synthesizer is going to assume; the set of tools available for synthesizing; the ways in which to produce and get feedback on interim drafts; and the particular criteria on which success is likely to be judged.

Since I believe that physicians should, at least on occasion, heal themselves, let me apply this recipe to the current chapter. My purpose has been to synthesize the existing knowledge on synthesis in order to inform aspiring synthesizers. The stance has been expository—a social-scientific analysis of why synthesis is important, along with proposals about the kinds of cognitive and motivational processes that are entailed in its achievement. I have addressed educators, professionals, and those in the business world. The tools have been a set of lists, garnished with examples drawn from disparate fields. Examples of more or less successful syntheses have been offered. The criteria for success should be provided by you, the consumer of the synthesis. I would expect that a worthy "synthesis on synthesis" should be clear, at least minimally original, reasonably convincing, and potentially useful.

So far, the examples that I have given could have been pursued at any time in recent centuries. The question arises about the extent to which technological tools will support synthesizing efforts in the future. Already in wide use are search engines that enable the user to track various topics and see how they have been related to one another. In the works are tools that allow one to look at one's own previous notes and ideas and to track how these have evolved over time.[15] To the extent that one can spell out the exact steps involved in synthesis, it should become possible to create software that executes this process as well as or better than most of us. I would not hold my breath, however, for computational aids that achieve what Kant or Leonardo did, using only a writing implement and their own considerable wit.

Test makers are beginning to explore synthesizing capacities. In a paradigm used with teaching candidates in France, the test taker is given the opportunity to study four passages on a topic (say, the historical transition from oracy to literacy); she is then asked to provide a succinct summary of points of agreement and disagreement in the texts, and to propose methods of instruction. In a prototype being developed by the Educational Testing Service, students are given a number of sources relevant to a product (e.g., tools usable by left-handed architects) and asked to summarize the data, evaluate the sources, and provide a rank order of their reliability. In an analogous instrument being developed by the Council for Aid to Education, candidates are given a set of documents about crime in a given county and asked to prepare a briefing paper for a mayoral candidate. While these attempts are driven more by empirical considerations than by any theory of synthesis, they should provide useful information for those of us who would like to understand better the processes whereby we human beings synthesize information for ourselves and others. And to the extent that these attempts prove predictive, they may come to be used by admissions officers, executives, recruiters, and human resource specialists.

MULTIPERSPECTIVALISM: AN INTERMEDIATE STEP

For a time, I maintained that genuine interdisciplinary work should await the mastery of disciplinary work. In the rush toward interdisciplinary gold, one runs a risk of integrations that are premature and, indeed, undisciplined. Given the growing importance of interdisciplinary work, however, and the current presses to encourage it—at least at the rhetorical level!—educators need to make sure that if it were done, it were done as well as possible.

In this context, I find useful the concept of *multiperspectivalism*. While the term may jar, the idea appears to be well motivated. A multiperspectival approach recognizes that different analytic perspectives can contribute to the elucidation of an issue or problem. While full-fledged disciplinary mastery may be an unattainable goal, individuals of most any age or specialization can reasonably be expected to appreciate the complementary strengths of different perspectives.

Take, for example, a high school course on Nazism. Secondary-school students cannot be expected to be scientific or historical disciplinarians. Neither the disciplinary knowledge nor the disciplinary tools will have been consolidated. Yet, these students are likely to acquire a better understanding of the rise of Nazism if they can appreciate the various perspectives that can be donned: genetic explanation of differences between populations, along with the various pseudoscientific claims made by eugenicists; historical explanation of the long-festering factors that created a fertile soil for Nazi beliefs and practices, as well as the contingent factors that led to the Nazis' surprising, largely lawful takeover of the German governmental apparatus in the early 1930s.

Enter multiperspectivalism. The process begins with a student listening to or monitoring disparate perspectives, such as those of the historian and the geneticist, as each attempts to explicate aspects of Nazism. In ensuing phases, the student is initially able to ask pertinent questions of the experts; next, to understand their answers; and ultimately, to provide answers (or, at least, the *types* of answers) that might be formulated, respectively, by a historian or a geneticist. To be sure, the secondary-school student can rarely contribute original knowledge of a historical or scientific sort. And yet, as one who is coming to appreciate the respective strengths of two or more perspectives, she is in a much stronger position to integrate or synthesize these strands of knowing.

The stance of multiperspectivalism proves especially illuminating at the workplace. It is unreasonable to expect that, thrown together for a time, doctors, nurses, therapists, and social workers should be able to master fully the expertise of the other professional roles. Remember the ten-year rule! By the same token, it is unreasonable to expect that, within a corporate context, the sales, marketing, creative, financial, and managerial types should all be able instantly to speak the same language. But if efforts are made to evolve an adequate pidgin, and if each practitioner at least learns to anticipate the concerns of colleagues from a different background, then the prospect of productive goal-directed teamwork is enhanced.

So far, I've spoken about multiperspectivalism in terms of complementary disciplinary backgrounds. But individuals also bring nondisciplinary perspectives to the table. Many projects are enhanced when individuals of different economic, social, ethnic, and/or racial backgrounds roll up their sleeves and work together to find solutions. Studies document that the opportunity to rub shoulders with individuals from significantly different backgrounds is one of the greatest benefits of life at select undergraduate schools.[16] Of course, sometimes such encounters produce clashes. Depending on how effectively they are handled, the clashes can be productive ... or they can be disastrous.

And what of genuine interdisciplinary thought? I consider it a relatively rare achievement, one that awaits mastery of at least the central components of two or more disciplines. In nearly all cases, such an achievement is unlikely before an individual has completed advanced studies. Yet, given the import of the issues that require interdisciplinary work, much effort will be devoted in coming years to nurturing of the interdisciplinary mind and to the delineation of experiences at school or the workplace that at least convey the power of interdisciplinary thinking. The Theory of Knowledge course, offered during the final year of the International Baccalaureate, represents one promising effort in this regard. Joint advanced degrees, in journalism and law, or in medicine and management, represent other potentially instructive models.

SYNTHESIZING TRACKS?

In the distant past, a comprehensive synthesizing mind seemed within reach. Knowledge accumulated far more gradually; wise persons like Aristotle and Leonardo had at least a rough grasp of the full panorama of knowledge. (The nineteenth-century English educator, scholar, and poet Matthew Arnold has been nominated as the last individual who could be said to have mastered all extant knowledge—to put it more colloquially, "to have known everything worth knowing.") While there was little formal inculcation of synthesizing capacities, the undergraduate regimen of liberal arts and the final year of college, in particular, when a capstone course was taught by the president, were seen as periods during which individuals were encouraged to find various connections among the fragments of knowledge that they had been accumulating. Perhaps the *consilience*—the unity of all scientific knowledge—about which biologist E. O. Wilson has admiringly written, is coming to replace the role once assumed by philosophical study.[17]

But we live in a time where our most talented minds know more and more about increasingly narrow spheres. The division of labor that Adam Smith noted in the marketplace of commerce has swept the marketplace of ideas as well. And there is no reason to expect that the drive toward specialization will be stemmed—or even that it would be a good idea to put the brakes on heightened "laser" disciplinary exploration.

I discern two primary antidotes. One involves training the range of individuals so that they can participate effectively in interdisciplinary groups. My sketch of the multidisciplinary or multiperspectival perspective is one possible model. Certainly, training institutions could experiment with structures and processes that foster understanding and cooperation among masters of different disciplines. I would not be surprised to learn of commercial software that promises to enhance synthesizing powers—though I'd ask for a money-back guarantee!

The second antidote entails the creation of educational programs directed specifically at certain individuals of promise—for example, leaders for tomorrow. Chief executives and general managers are expected to be able to see the big picture—to look beyond their own background and specialization; to understand the various components in their organization or constituency; to think systemically about what is working, what is not working, and how goals can be more effectively achieved. Programs that enhance their synthesizing capacities—and that yoke synthesizing and strategizing—would be valuable, and one can expect that various consulting firms will offer such a menu of options. Other individuals—for example, those exhibiting a "searchlight" or "bricoleur" intelligence—might be attracted to such programs as well. They could make use of their enhanced skills even if they do not occupy explicit leadership roles. Perhaps, as educator Vartan Gregorian has suggested, we need a specialization in becoming a generalist.[18] Such a specialization would target promising candidates and devote resources toward the enhancement of synthesizing capacities.

Neither of these interventions is likely to be effective, however, unless two conditions prevail. On the one hand, we need role models—individuals who are themselves gifted at multiperspectivalism, interdisciplinarity, and/or synthesizing. In recent years, Jacob Bronowski, Stephen Jay Gould, and E. O. Wilson have elegantly filled that role in biology; in the sphere of management, Andy Grove at Intel, John Browne at BP, John Reed at Citicorp, and Bill Gates at Microsoft are often cited as examples of individuals with wide knowledge and admirable synthesizing or integrating capacities. Bill Clinton, an outstanding synthesizer, recently reflected on this capacity: "I think intellect is a good thing unless it paralyzes your ability to make decisions because you see too much complexity. Presidents need to have what I would call a synthesizing intelligence."[19]

But along with exemplary paragons, we also need criteria that establish the differences between excellent, adequate, and inappropriate integrations. And we must accept that these criteria are mission- or topic-specific. What counts as a good synthesis in evolutionary biology may differ markedly from an integration that is appropriate for the arts or commerce. A synthesis suitable for determining the limits of complexity theory may bear little resemblance to a synthesis adequate for addressing the eradication of poverty or the control of the AIDS epidemic.

Some syntheses will be straightforward; some will involve a stretch of one sort or another; perhaps the most precious ones involve a creative leap. To the cultivation of the creative mind, we now turn.

CHAPTER **4**

The Creating Mind

IN OUR GLOBAL, wired society, creativity is sought after, culti-vated, praised. Corporate visionary John Seely Brown has quipped that, in the world of tomorrow, people will say, "I create; therefore I am." When I give talks about intelligence, I am routinely asked about how to nurture creativity. Audiences expect that I will fully endorse creativity and hope that I will (for all time and without charging!) reveal the secret of its attainment.

It was not always so. In most human societies, throughout most of human history, creativity was neither sought after nor rewarded. Just as human beings have a conservative bent, one that militates against educational innovation and interdisciplinary leaps, human societies also strive to maintain their current form. We are stunned by the achievements of ancient Egyptian society but conveniently forget that the society evolved at a glacial pace. We honor innova-tive scientists like Galilei Galileo but need to be reminded that Galileo was denounced and imprisoned and that Giordano Bruno, his scientific forefather, was burned at the stake. Neither Johann Se-bastian Bach nor Vincent van Gogh nor Gregor Mendel received much appreciation during their lifetimes—and Freud, Darwin, and Keynes received their share of ridicule (more than their share, they might insist!).

In the past, creative individuals in a society were at best a mixed blessing—disdained, discouraged, even destroyed at the time of their breakthroughs, possibly to be honored by posterity at some later point. Our time, our era is different. Almost every task that can be routinized will be, probably sooner rather than later. (Perhaps in fifty years' time, a book like this will be written—and perhaps read as well for pleasure or self-improvement—by a quantum computer.) Virtually all innovation can be communicated almost instantly the world over, available to be built on by anyone with the requisite disciplinary skills, understanding, and motivation. And while most innovations will have a short half-life, those that address a pressing need or fulfill a genuine ardor will spread very quickly and last long. In the technological realm, think of the rapid successes of the telephone, the automobile, the airplane; and in more recent years, the personal computer, the videogame, the Internet, the cell phone, the iPod, the BlackBerry. Think as well of the rise of fast foods, the spread of fashion sneakers, the veneration of pop stars Elvis or Madonna, Brad or Angelina (no last names necessary in 2006!). Those corporations that do not embrace innovation will almost inevitably be muscled out by those that do. Indeed, insufficient attention to innovation may be the principal reason that many of the leading American corporations of fifty years ago (think Sears Roebuck, American Motors, Pan American Airlines, Westinghouse) have either shrunk in size or gone out of business altogether.

CREATIVITY RECONCEPTUALIZED

Viewed most broadly, creation is part and parcel of the fabric of the world. While many of us no longer believe literally in the biblical story of creation, we recognize that the world is populated by living creatures and living creations, each at least a bit different from the rest. By definition, all human artifacts are initially created by someone. Whether when one thinks of biological or artifactual or conceptual entities, the most appealing "mutants" are most likely to survive and propagate.

Early views of creativity stressed either the role of the divine, or the roll of the dice. Those who formulated theories of creation favored the notion that certain individuals were touched with mysterious inspiration, though occasional iconoclasts (like American poet Edgar Allan Poe) claimed that human creation proceeded according to a strict, explicable, logical formula. Within psychology, views of creativity tended to follow views of intelligence—by a lag of about fifty years. Until recently, creativity has been seen by psychologists as a trait of certain individuals; as such, it should be measurable through paper-and-pencil tests; and an individual deemed "creative" should be able to evince that trait across various performance domains. In the prototypical item on a creativity test, subjects are asked to think of as many uses as possible for a paper clip, or to give an imaginative title to a squiggle, or to choose the target that can be associated with two supplied words (mouse-cottage: both can be linked to cheese). The final tally received on such a measure is believed to reflect creative potential in any domain of knowledge.

This way of thinking about creativity migrated to the world of business. Perhaps the chief guru has been Edward de Bono, the polymath from Malta. De Bono has emphasized the importance of *lateral thinking*—the capacity to shift frameworks, wear different hats, come up with a plethora of ingenious solutions to a nagging dilemma.[1] De Bono deserves credit for highlighting the importance of thinking about thinking—"metathinking" if you will—and for coming up with any number of intriguing problems and offbeat solutions. Yet, his perspective on creativity as a generalizable capacity that can be quickly boosted has distinct limitations.

Accordingly, in recent years, a number of social scientists have adopted a different viewpoint. To begin with, we recognize a variety of relatively independent creative endeavors. A creator can solve a hitherto vexing problem (like the structure of DNA), formulate a new conundrum or theory (like string theory in physics), fashion a work in a genre, or perform online in real or mock battle (deciding to buy or sell a volatile stock). The problem-solution couplet represents but one type of creative thought; moreover, skill in one variety need not entail skill in other creative endeavors. (A creative mathematician can be an execrable debater—or vice versa.) We also recognize a range of creative achievements—from the little *c* involved in a new floral arrangement to the big *C* entailed in the theory of relativity. And, most important, we do not assume that a person creative in one realm (say, Wolfgang Amadeus Mozart or Virginia Woolf) could have switched places with a person creative in another realm (say, Diego Velasquez or Marie Curie). Each of these assumptions collides with the one-size-of-creativity-fits-all view proposed by standard psychology and popularized by Edward de Bono.

A most important insight, due to psychologist Mihaly Csikszentmihalyi, is the realization that creativity is never simply the achievement of a lone individual or even a small group. Rather, creativity is the occasional emergent from the interaction of three autonomous elements:

1. The *individual* who has mastered some discipline or domain of practice and is steadily issuing variations in that domain (e.g., the historian penning a series of history essays, a composer issuing musical scores, a software engineer writing programs, and the like).

2. The cultural *domain* in which an individual is working, with its models, prescriptions, and proscriptions (the specifications for a scholarly paper, a musical score, a program in HTML or Flash).

3. The social *field*—those individuals and institutions that provide access to relevant educational experiences as well as opportunities to perform. Representatives of the field ultimately pass judgment on the merit of the individual and/or his candidate creation(s). (Representatives of the field include admissions officers, judges of competitions, patent officers, authors of textbooks and encyclopedias, and the editors or publishers who permit or thwart publication.) Of course, in the world of commerce, the ultimate field is the consumer.[2]

According to Csikszentmihalyi, creativity occurs when—and only when—an individual or group product generated in a particular domain is recognized by the relevant field as innovative and, in turn, sooner or later, exerts a genuine, detectable influence on subsequent work in that domain. This perspective applies to the full range of creations, across spheres and across varying degrees of innovation (from the littlest c to the biggest C). For example, in 1900, a number of prominent physicists and mathematicians were wrestling with unresolved issues about the nature of light, gravity, time, space. Each disciplinary master was offering theoretical formulations and empirical conjectures. Working in relative isolation, an unknown patent officer named Albert Einstein wrote a number of innovative papers. Until the merit of these papers had been recognized by editors and other knowledgeable colleagues, however, it was not possible to tell whether Einstein's work was simply atypical or truly important. The same story can be told about the writings of James Joyce; the paintings of Pablo Picasso; the managerial strategies developed by Alfred P. Sloan, Michael Porter, and Peter Drucker; the musical compositions of Richard Wagner, Duke Ellington, and John Lennon; the economic theories of John Maynard Keynes and Milton Friedman. Indeed, the acid test for creativity is simply stated: has the domain in which you operate been significantly altered by your contribution? The good news: because there is no statute of limitations, you can never know for sure that you have *not* been creative!

FROM COMPUTATION TO CHARACTER

Clearly, the aspiring creator needs a generous supply of intelligence(s), skill, and discipline. Shakespeare was a genius in language and equally brilliant in his understanding of the human condition; the trajectory of growth from his earliest writings to his most mature plays is stunning. Still, that trajectory spans a twenty-year period. Mozart had remarkable musical gifts from early childhood. Even so, the works from his first decade of composing (up to age fifteen!) are mostly curiosities. But by late adolescence, he had already become a world-class composer. John Maynard Keynes was recognized early for his prodigious mind; yet he did not publish his masterwork, *The General Theory of Employment, Interest, and Money*, until he was in his early fifties.[3]

For every talented writer or composer who breaks new ground, however, hundreds are content—or resigned—to be "mere" experts. An expert is an individual who, after a decade or more of training, has reached the pinnacle of current practice in her chosen domain. The world depends on experts. And, indeed, when it comes to surgery or airplane flight or bookkeeping, we are well advised to consult an expert and to be leery of the innovator.

How, then, does the creator differ from the expert? In my view, the difference is not principally cognitive, at least not cognitive in the usual sense of the term. Tested on mastery of a domain, both kinds of individuals should perform equally well. (During his time, few believed that Mozart was a more talented composer than Karl Ditters von Dittersdorf, or the more infamous—if less euphonious—Antonio Salieri.) Intriguingly, prodigies in a domain rarely turn out to be creators. Since early childhood prodigies have been rewarded for doing precisely what the adults in their domain were doing; and so it requires a remaking of self—a sharp change in goals, orientation, and motivation—to set off in new, uncharted directions. A wit said of Camille Saint-Saëns, an aging musical prodigy who never fully realized his early promise: "He has everything but he lacks inexperience."

The creator stands out in terms of temperament, personality, and stance. She is perennially dissatisfied with current work, current standards, current questions, current answers. She strikes out in unfamiliar directions and enjoys—or at least accepts—being different from the pack. When an anomaly arises (an unfamiliar musical chord, an unexpected experimental result, a spike or dip in the sale of goods in an unfamiliar territory), she does not shrink from that unexpected wrinkle: indeed, she wants to understand it and to determine whether it constitutes a trivial error, an unrepeatable fluke, or an important but hitherto unknown truth. She is tough skinned and robust. There is a reason why so many famous creators hated or dropped out of school—they did not like marching to someone else's tune (and, in turn, the authorities disliked their idiosyncratic marching patterns).

All of us fail, and—because they are bold and ambitious—creators fail the most frequently and, often, the most dramatically. Only a person who is willing to pick herself up and "try and try again" is likely to forge creative achievements. And even when an achievement has been endorsed by the field, the prototypical creator rarely rests on her laurels; instead, she proceeds along a new, untested path, fully ready to risk failure time and again in return for the opportunity to make another, different mark. Creative activity harbors more than its share of heartaches; but the "flow" that accompanies a fresh insight, a breakthrough work, or a genuine invention can be addictive.

EDUCATING THE CREATOR ACROSS
THE AGE SPAN

From these formulations, an educational regimen follows. It deviates from the trajectory of the disciplinarian approach, though it bears similarities to the emergence of the synthesizer. An individual on a strict disciplinary track masters the key literacies; as soon as practical, she commences a regular and systematic mastery of disciplines like mathematics, science, and history. She will presumably become an expert in short order (read: a decade). But too strict an adherence to a disciplinary track operates against the more open stances of the synthesizer or the creator. Options need to be kept open—a straight trajectory is less effective than one entailing numerous bypaths, and even a few disappointing but instructive cul-de-sacs.

Members of one age group need little pressure to assume the creative stance—young children before the age of formal schooling. Given even a modestly supportive environment, youngsters are not only intrigued by a wide range of phenomena, experiences, topics, and questions; they persist in exploring, even in the absence of encouragement, let alone material rewards. Few are the children who are not galvanized by a trip to a county fair, an amusement park, or a children's museum; their playfulness, curiosity, and imaginative powers are palpable. The mind of the five-year-old represents, in one sense, the height of creative powers.

Accordingly, the challenge to the educator is to keep alive the mind and the sensibility of the young child. Artists and scientists have always known this: Pablo Picasso famously declared, "I used to draw like Raphael; it has taken me my whole life to learn to draw like a child."[4] With equal conviction (and equal quotability), Isaac Newton reflected, "To myself, I seem to have been only like a boy playing on the seashore and diverting myself in now and then finding a smoother pebble or a prettier shell than ordinary while the great ocean of truth lay all undiscovered before me."

But how to retain a childlike sensibility—what embryologists term *neoteny*—throughout life? So much depends on the messages that exist outside the walls of the school and, for that matter, within the classrooms that serve the mass of children. This point was brought home to me sharply during the 1980s, when I made a number of trips to China and visited dozens of classrooms in several cities.[5] At the time, China was still traumatized by the disastrous Cultural Revolution (1966–1976), and considerable fearfulness gripped the populace. In just about every area of competence, teachers clung to a depressingly constrained notion of what it meant to be an excellent student. From a very early age, young children's behavior was strictly molded along a path designed to yield the expert calligrapher, musician, dancer, mathematician, and the like. Deviations from the disciplinary prototype were strongly discouraged—step-by-step, error-free learning was the preferred route. In a society like China circa 1980, models and experiences of a more open-ended, more creative sort were rare. And so, in addressing Chinese colleagues, I would have encouraged—indeed, I *did* encourage—a regimen that featured exploration, challenging problems, and the tolerance, if not the active encouragement, of productive mistakes.

At the time, China and the United States represented polar opposites. On the street, messages of creativity were rampant in the United States of the go-go eighties—in business, the media, technology, the arts. Everyone wanted to be creative: too many persons believed that they *were* creative, even though they had scarcely begun to master a domain, and even though no expert in the field would have judged them as creative. In schools (and in after-school sites), the compelling need was for the achievement of genuine mastery of a recognized discipline: not only was there no need for educators to wave the flag of creativity; it might even have been counterproductive to do so. Only through the honing of discipline would genuinely creative options ultimately emerge.

Today, of course, China and the United States have moved toward one another, and both are probably more representative of the patterns found around the rest of the globe. There are lots of models of creativity on the streets of major Chinese cities (not to mention Internet links that constantly defy the censors); moreover, due to the influence of economically successful societies in East Asia, the curriculum has become a bit more receptive to the arts, choice, the posing of open-ended questions, and the acceptance of a variety of responses to those questions. (Note, however, that the sinological pendulum of permissiveness continues to swing back and forth, as it has for centuries.) In contrast, in the United States of the early twenty-first century, the messages for creativity endure on the streets, but schools have taken a sharply conservative turn. The United States has moved toward uniform curricula, tests, and standards, while progressively tinted education (which I personally favor) is on the defensive.

Accordingly, a generic formula can be put forth for the nurturing of creating minds in the first decades of life. Following a period of open, untrammeled exploration in early childhood, it is indeed appropriate to master literacies and the disciplines. However, even during periods of drill, it is vital to keep open alternative possibilities and to foreground the option of unfettered exploration. Sluices of creativity can be maintained by exhibiting different, equally viable solutions to a single posed problem; exposing youngsters to attractive, creative persons who model both the approach and the experiences of the creative life; and introducing new pursuits that are removed from the academic treadmill and that reward innovation and look benignly on errors. (As Internet guru Esther Dyson quips, "Make *new* mistakes!") More concretely, in the years of middle childhood, parents should make sure that their children pursue hobbies or activities that do not feature a single right answer. Teachers ought to illustrate the several ways in which a particular math problem can properly be solved or a literary passage can be interpreted; they ought to facilitate classroom visits by charismatic inventors and artists who have gone their own way and achieved success; they ought to encourage youngsters to play games drawn from other cultures or to invent new games on the playground or on the computer.

As I pointed out in my discussion of the synthesizing mind, it is advantageous to develop multiple, diverse representations of the same entity—be it arithmetic multiplication, the nature of political revolution, the current competitive landscape in one's business, the topography of one's hometown, the contours of one's own life. Such multiple representations are grist for new ways of thinking about an entity, problem, or question: they catalyze creative questions and spawn creative solutions. How much more likely is the ten-year-old to make money in her neighborhood if she thinks about a variety of needs, products, and modes of exchange.

As students enter adolescence, they become capable of envisioning possibilities that are quite different from—and may, indeed, invert—their current realities. (I am not speaking here about devouring the *Harry Potter* series; I am alluding to the capacity to appreciate how certain givens in one's own society—say, the legal system—could be fundamentally transformed.) Especially in those settings where such envisioning has not been encouraged, elders have a responsibility to introduce instances and systems that operate according to different rules—utopias, dystopias, alternative numerical systems, counterfactual historical accounts, competing economic systems, and the like. The adolescent mind can take it from there.

If the mind of the young child is charmingly uncritical, the mind of the adolescent is often overly critical—of self and of other. Such hypercriticism can thwart creative efforts. No less than creative faculties, critical faculties need to be honed. In part, this process can be launched in the preadolescent years, when criticism may not sting so sharply. During adolescence and thereafter, students need to be posed challenges where they stand a reasonable chance of success; they should practice giving and receiving criticism that is constructive; they should learn which criticisms are worth attending to and which are better ignored. Only a masochist craves criticism; but the rest of us must learn to deal with it and, as much as possible, to internalize and anticipate criticism, so that we may ultimately become our first and our sharpest critics. Often, I have observed, these dispositions are developed more readily in art classes than in the standard college-prep curriculum. The disappearance of the arts from many curricula may have unintended negative consequences.

In some domains, like mathematics, chess, and lyric poetry, the heights of creativity tend to be reached early in the adult years. In others, the developmental path to mastery is much longer, but perhaps in compensation, achievements continue to be possible for decades. Philosophers, historians, musical conductors, diplomats, religious leaders, and psychoanalysts go on and on and on. The same can be said of some business leaders—in the year 2006, octogenarians Sumner Redstone and Sidney Harman, and septuagenarians Warren Buffet and Rupert Murdoch come to mind. Those who make fundamental discoveries early in life must somehow retain or regain their early innocence; metaphorically speaking, they must remain youths. Freud once observed, "When I was young, ideas came to me; as I age, I must go halfway to meet them." As the average life span increases, creators (and the societies that value them) will search for new ways—perhaps psychological, perhaps physiological—to retain youthful minds and to catalyze irreverent stances.

What of the fostering of creativity at the workplace? Nowadays, few workplaces worthy of the name would do anything but proclaim themselves as cradles of creativity. Nor do I deny their avowed intentions. But as psychologist Teresa Amabile has amply demonstrated, too many corporations do not have the courage of their convictions.[6] In ways large and small, they signal that too much originality—be it in dress, political views, or business sagacity—is taboo: too expensive, too risky, too divisive. Conventionality is rewarded; deviants are marginalized or fired. Yet other businesses "solve" the problem by spinning off creativity—relegating it to Skunk Works, or allowing only the most recently acquired divisions to march to their own drummer. Experience shows that this divide-and-conquer strategy rarely lasts—if creativity does not infiltrate the DNA of an organization, it is unlikely to be passed on to the next generation. Of course, inappropriate creativity in accounting and financing can be suicidal, as Arthur Andersen and Enron learned shortly after the turn of the century.[7]

The incorporation of creative DNA has occurred over the decades in a few model companies such as 3M. This admired company fills its senior ranks with individuals who are proven creators. Promotions and rewards are offered to individuals who come up with new ideas. The leadership team works closely with "early adapters" and "ingenious users," tapping their ideas and giving them commensurate rewards. Management gives a lot of slack to those who think outside the box. Executives realize at a deep level that creativity is a chancy undertaking that can never be guaranteed—only fostered or thwarted.

Another company obsessed with innovation is General Electric. Under the legendary leadership of Jack Welch, GE went into a whole variety of new businesses and implemented radical methods for promoting the most outstanding product lines and individuals while excising those that did not assume leadership positions. Welch's successor, Jeffrey Immelt, realizes that the next generation of innovation must take place chiefly within the current portfolio of GE holdings.[8] Accordingly, he is leading a search for themes like eco-imagination that cut across the entire company, and for "enterprise" sales approaches that offer a suite of goods and services to an institution, like a hospital, or to a blockbuster event, like the Olympics. Immelt has also set aside $1 billion a year for R&D. He hopes for a thousand breakthrough ideas rather than a hundred, with a special premium on those ideas that can find resonance in different sections of this multi-industry, multinational corporation.

Occasionally, a wholly new form of business is created. Before the age of the Internet, commerce generally took place face-to-face or through well-established intermediaries, like shopping catalogs or purchasing agents. Once it became possible for any two individuals or entities to be in touch with one another instantaneously, to interact at will for as many volleys as necessary, and to have access to essentially infinite amounts of relevant information, new options opened up. Especially in a nation like the United States, which is friendly to entrepreneurship and recently has had available generous dollops of venture capital, many hundreds of new businesses emerged, each trying in its own, often secretive, way to take advantage of the potentials of the new medium. The United States of the late 1990s was a hotbed of creativity in action.

Then came a bitter shakedown in the period 2000–2001, and suddenly most of those businesses—several thousand by one estimate—were no more. And quite a few others that had been touted as the waves of the future were either diminished in scope (like Priceline) or found themselves reverting to their central, more traditional business core (like Cisco).

It is by no means clear that, in 1995 or even 2000, one could have predicted which of the Internet-based businesses would be riding high in the middle of the first decade of the new millennium. Amazon, Google, and eBay have each had their ups and downs. Yet, at least in retrospect, one can see how each succeeded in identifying a fundamental human desire and in using the Internet ingeniously to fill that need—in present terms, how they identified a crucial domain and created a receptive field.

Starting with the sale of publications, and moving into all manners of goods and services, Amazon made it easy to buy these products while seated at the computer and provided all kinds of user-based feedback to aid in making one's purchase. Amazon knows which books I would like to own as well as do my friends and families; and it tells the world what other people think of books I have written, even when I'd prefer if the site were to exercise the delete option.

Google responds to the human desire to get information as quickly and reliably as possible—and for free! One need only type in the information that is needed, and a huge number of relevant resources are placed at one's disposable. Initially, sources were ordered strictly in terms of frequency of use, but now Google experts are employing more nuanced measures of quality. On the horizon are plans to digitize all books ever written and to use computer programs that understand requests well enough to be able to provide meaningful responses. Graders of term papers, beware!

EBay is the ultimate shopper's paradise: an electronic bazaar where one can purchase just about anything, or sell just about anything; the user has the ability to make bids, accept them, or reject them. The procedures devised to consummate the purchase are efficient, reliable, and trustworthy. And one can ascertain the reliability of the person—though not, revealingly, the person's real name—with whom one is dealing, because users grade the performance of other users. EBay has also accomplished the considerable feat of creating a community—all over the world, users of eBay feel a bond to one another. And while the handlers of eBay are inclined toward hyperbole on the subject, it is fair to say that the community exhibits a generous amount of self-governance. EBay has created an impressive blend of market-driven mechanisms and democratic procedures. Its openness stands in sharp contrast to the obsessive secrecy that led to the rise of Enron and to Enron's ultimate undoing.

To be sure, generating the creative idea is only part of the story. All sorts of things can go wrong in proceeding from novel idea to effective business. Each of the aforementioned companies has had or acquired skilled management, and each has been willing to make difficult choices and sharp changes of direction when circumstances dictated those moves. Each has also been involved in expensive litigation, sometimes against other creators of the Internet landscape. Each is ever on the lookout for ways of expanding its business: as leading success stories of the Internet age, each has the license to broaden its ambit of operation and to challenge its chief competitor on its home turf. Each promotes creativity in its employees and its users: Google, for example, gives employees a day a week to work on projects that are not directly linked to revenue. And, finally, each is ever alert to the next, so-called killer application that could threaten to undermine its hegemony in the marketplace—maybe even before you have read these lines! Creative breakthroughs do not last forever.

CREATIVITY BY GROUPS, LARGE AND SMALL

Except in the area of business, most studies of creativity, and most students of creativity, have focused on the minds, the methods, and the motivations of the individual creator. This bias reflects the interest of psychologists, on the one hand, and the romance associated with individual inventive personalities, on the other. Creativity by dyads, trios, or larger groups is seen as anomalous, or simply as the sum of the capacities of the individual members of these groups.

The limits of this focus on the individual are becoming clear. In the sciences—be it particle physics or genomics—a great deal of the most important work is carried on by huge teams, often numbering many hundreds. Artistic productions on the stage or on the screen also involve large ensembles of personalities, often creative, often prickly, often clashing. In the period of mass media, the potential of a work to appeal to millions of persons is at a premium; and sometimes the plug is pulled on a huge work involving representatives of several arts and crafts, if early signs suggest that it will fail to appeal to a sufficiently wide audience. In the area of management consultancy, teams swoop down on a company in crisis, trouble-shoot, and then issue their report and their recommendations. I call these kinds of collaborations "Hollywood-style"; large numbers of persons, often unknown to one another, must come together over brief periods of time, make the necessary connections, and trust one another to complete the job efficiently and move on to the next assignment—be it making a movie sequel or advising another corporation.

Yet another form of group creativity has recently coalesced—the wisdom of crowds. We see this phenomenon at work in the Google sources that are most popular, the Amazon books that are recommended, the eBay sellers who are most trusted. Open source programming, where dozens of individuals may make contributions to a computer program, is another, often touted instance. Perhaps the clearest—and one of the most controversial—examples is Wikipedia. This twist on the traditional encyclopedia features entries that are originally posted by one or more authors, and then subjected to as many rewrites—and, one hopes, as many improvements—as there are individuals prepared to spend time researching the topic and contributing new verbiage.

The question arises about whether ideas about creativity need to be refashioned to take into account the increasing number of projects and realms where the individual contribution seems less critical, the group mind more crucial. Clearly, the abilities to come to know individuals quickly, to forge a working relationship, to handle issues of conflict and credit, take on added importance. Brainstorming and improvisation come to the fore; personal glory recedes in importance.

My own take on this issue involves a recognition of a continuum. At one end of the continuum, one finds a deep societal issue like the causes of poverty or the pervasiveness of racism, one not open to ready formulation or solution. Solutions offered by the public at large are unlikely to be helpful. In contrast, at the other end of the continuum are issues that reflect the wishes or interest of a particular cohort or of the community at large: in such cases, contributions on the part of many heterogeneous individuals may well be the preferred route. We can apply this metric to encyclopedias: if we want to know about the appeal of Elvis Presley or *American Idol*, we might turn to Wikipedia; if we want to understand Kant's contributions, we are better advised to read a contribution by a recognized authority in the *Britannica*.

I can add a personal example. Several times in my life, Harvard University has selected a president. When it comes to arriving at a short list, the wisdom of the crowd will be superior to that of any individual nominator. When, however, a decision about the final choice is due, majority vote is no substitute for consulted judgment and wisdom on the part of the most knowledgeable insiders—and the most knowledgeable outsiders.

Even at the "deep problem" end of the continuum, options exist. Some problems and projects are handled better by a small group of individuals who know one another well and who work together regularly over a long period of time. Such shop talk happens in established scientific laboratories, repertory companies, string quartets. Other problems and projects can be handled equally well by groups that are brought together on an *ad hoc* basis: the latter option permits the commissioning of individuals who have the precise talent that is needed, fosters diverse views, and militates against groupthink or falling into a rut.

CREATIVITY GONE AWRY

Of course, the risk of "dangerous" or "feigned" or "false" creativity always lurks in the background. Enron proclaimed itself one of the most innovative companies in the world. And indeed, what Enron purported to do in the 1990s—to deal with futures in the gas industry, to place orders and trade on the Internet, to oversee the privatization of power in many developing nations—represented uncharted pathways in the energy industry. The problem, we all now know, was that much of the so-called creativity was pseudocreativity—based on false estimates, hopes rather than data, and good (correction: bad) old-fashioned criminality.

Nor is the realm of science immune from false instances of creativity or, if you prefer, instances of false creativity. Take the realm of the physical sciences. In the seventeenth and eighteenth centuries, the conventional wisdom stipulated that substances burned because they contained an element called "phlogiston," a tasteless, colorless substance that was given off during the process of burning until the substance was "dephlogisticated." But phlogiston turned out to be an invention of chemists who were trying to account for a process that they did not understand. Thanks to investigations by Antoine Lavoisier, scientists came to appreciate that combustion occurred when substances (like a fuel) combined with oxygen and reached a certain temperature.

A similar unmasking occurred one hundred years ago. Throughout the nineteenth century, physicists posited a medium called "the ether," through which all manner of light and heat waves were thought to pass. It was left to the experiments of Albert Michelson and Edward Morley, and the theoretical acumen of Albert Einstein, to prove that—like phlogiston—the ether did not exist. Any model of the universe that it implied was superfluous.

Not just our ancestors can be seriously mistaken. One of the most notable claims in recent decades was the highly touted discovery of cold fusion. On March 23, 1989, at a hastily called news conference, Stanley Pons and Martin Fleischmann, two well-known physicists at the University of Utah, announced that they had achieved a remarkable feat. At room temperature, they had compressed heavy atoms of hydrogen inside cold fusion cells: the cells consisted of two metal electrodes, one palladium and one platinum, dipped in a jar of heavy water spiked with lithium salt and connected to a moderate electrode current. The resulting fusion supposedly released a huge amount of energy, an amount that had previously been associated only with "hot" nuclear reactions at very high temperatures. According to the press release issued at the time, "[T]wo scientists have successfully created a sustained nuclear fusion reaction at room temperature in a chemistry laboratory at the University of Utah. The breakthrough means the world may someday rely on fusion for a clean, virtually inexhaustible source of energy."[9]

This announcement, relayed immediately by the media throughout the world, caused a sensation. The *Wall Street Journal* declared that "scientists working at the University of Utah made an unprecedented claim to have achieved a sustained hydrogen fusion reaction, thereby harnessing in the laboratory the fusion power of the hydrogen bomb. The two scientists said that with no more equipment than might be used in freshman chemistry class, they had triggered a fusion reaction in a test tube that continued for more than 100 hours."[10] It appeared as if essentially unlimited amount of cheap, safe, and clean energy could become available through a simple electrochemical process. Were this claim true, the need for fossil fuels, and the search for hitherto untapped energy sources like those from the sea or the sun, would be unnecessary. A consumer's paradise, at long last.

What happened in the ensuing months was instructive, especially for students of the creative process. Large amounts of governmental and private money were channeled into this line of research, both in the United States and abroad. A smattering of laboratories claimed that they had achieved similar demonstrations. This group, representatives of which persist to this day, might be considered "true believers." However, an ever larger proportion of the scientific community concluded that the claims of cold fusion were simply false. A few experts rejected the claims *a priori*—out of hand—indicating that the alleged findings flew in the face of our well-established understandings of how matter works. Several other leading experimentalists attempted unsuccessfully to replicate the results and became skeptical of the claims *a posteriori*.

Any claim to be creative occurs within a domain—traditional or newly constituted—and the criteria for ascertaining creativity are critical in rendering a judgment. Pons and Fleischmann were scientists, and their mettle came under severe attack. On scrutiny it emerged that their experiments had not been carried out carefully; the data had been reported incompletely and sloppily; obvious control conditions had not been instituted; indeed, the investigators had made their announcement prematurely, because they were afraid of being scooped by rival scientists at nearby Brigham Young University. Pushed for more details about their studies, so that others could understand and attempt to replicate their results, the two scholars became defensive and offensive. Perhaps most damning, they did not even offer a convincing explanation of *why* they had obtained the results that they claimed to have obtained. Science evolved—or degenerated—into politics. The phenomenon of cold fusion slowly went the way of phlogiston and the ether. Creativity gave way to sleight of hand.

A number of books have been written about the cold fusion episode.[11] Most are critical, though a few still see hope in the line of work pioneered—or perhaps better, popularized—by Pons and Fleischmann. I see the episode as a trademark example of creativity undermined by lack of discipline. Pons and Fleischmann were acknowledged scientists, well respected in their field. I am willing to give them the benefit of the doubt and to grant that their search for cold fusion was motivated by scientific curiosity and that their initial results were sufficiently promising to warrant further investigation.

Once they felt they were on to something of societal significance, however, the Utah researchers lost perspective. Rather than retaining the skepticism of scientists, rather than listening to the doubts that were raised by colleagues (some of whom were initially quite sympathetic to Pons and Fleishmann), the two scientists forgot the core values of their discipline: a search for the way that things actually operate, a respect for the peer review process, a willingness to share methods and findings, a humility that allows one to say that one was mistaken, that one had misinterpreted or overinterpreted the data. In our terms, they forgot about the domain in which they were working, ignored input from the relevant field, and tried to create a new field of naive boosters. Their failure ruined careers of university administrators, discredited young scientists in their own and in other errant laboratories, and, not least, undermined their own professional standing.

One might object that Pons and Fleischmann were creative but just had the bad luck to be wrong. I disagree. While anything goes in the generation of new ideas, the would-be creator has an obligation to be scrupulous in the completion and validation of work. Undisciplined creativity is creativity undermined. Even if Pons and Fleischmann should prove one day to have been correct in their hypotheses, they should not receive credit for the creative breakthrough. As for the proponents of phlogiston and the ether, it is probably better not to judge them in terms of their fidelity to unnecessary constructs, but rather in terms of their positive contributions, if any, to the science of their time.

CREATING AND SYNTHESIZING

Evidently, parallels abound between the synthesizing and the creating minds. To begin with, both require a baseline of literacy and discipline. Both benefit from the provision of multiple examples, exposure to multiple role models, and the construction of multiple representations of the same general topic. Indeed, no sharp line separates synthesis from creation. Some of the best creations emerge from attempts at synthesis (or synthesis gone awry); and, particularly among experts in training or scholars at the end of their active careers, a synthesis may represent a considerable creative achievement.

Yet, the impulses behind these two mental stances are distinctive. The synthesizer's goal is to place what has already been established in as useful and illuminating a form as possible. The creator's goal, on the other hand, is to extend knowledge, to ruffle the contours of a genre, to guide a set of practices along new and hitherto unanticipated directions. The synthesizer seeks order, equilibrium, closure; the creator is motivated by uncertainty, surprise, continual challenge, and disequilibrium. We may appropriate a famous distinction put forth by Friedrich Nietzsche. The synthesizer is Apollonian; possessed of a restrained temperament, she proceeds in a harmonious, balanced fashion. In contrast, the creator is Dionysian; of a tempestuous nature, she is poised to wrestle with the gods.

No society can be composed solely of creators; they are by nature destabilizing. History suggests that the "hotter" the creative center, the more rapidly it is likely to spend or extinguish itself. In 1900, Vienna was a center of creative thought; 50 or 100 years later, it would not appear on anyone's list. Yet there is little question that, for the foreseeable future, those societies that know how to nurture and sustain creativity—of both the little-c and the big-C varieties—are more likely to thrive than those that discourage creativity or those that are restricted to copying what genuine innovators have already achieved and what their successors are likely to surpass tomorrow.

How does the relation between synthesizing and creating play itself out in different settings? In the world of scholarship, it is expected that individuals will have achieved skill in synthesis before they venture into new arenas. At the graduate school where I teach, for example, one often writes a literature review as a qualifying paper; then, once the lit review has passed, one is allowed to write a dissertation, which (unlike the review) is assumed to be an original contribution to the same subdomain. Still, it is clear that certain experts in the making have the creative urge, while many others do not, or are ambivalent about stepping out on a limb. In the arts nowadays, synthesis plays a smaller role than it did in times past. Bach and Mozart saw themselves as masters of a tradition; John Cage and Igor Stravinsky saw tradition as something to be overthrown. Sheer novelty itself is often honored, though perhaps more in the short run than over the long haul. In corporate settings, synthesizing capacities are vital for both managers and leaders, with the leader expected to assume a wider purview in terms of both time span and terrain.

At the level of leadership, the 360-degree searchlight mind is generally more valued than the focused acute-angle laser mind. Even so, it is acknowledged that the most innovative products, sales, or marketing ideas are likely to come from those with a proclivity toward laser thinking—working alone or in consort. Only the rare leader—the transformative or visionary leader—displays genuine creativity. We see this creativity at work when subsequent generations enjoy the fruits and/or suffer the destructions of that leader—be it Napoléon or Mao Zedong, Queen Elizabeth I or Margaret Thatcher.

THREE GUISES OF CREATIVITY IN THE FUTURE

Until this point, the nurturance of creativity has been a human-centered enterprise. A critical mass of persons engaged in creative activity—Athens in the fifth century BC, Florence in the Renaissance, Vienna and Paris in 1900, Silicon Valley in the 1990s—constitutes the optimal formula for ensuring continuing innovation. Sociologist Richard Florida points to certain contemporary urban centers in America—Austin, San Diego, Seattle—that have emerged because they attract individuals who are young, comfortable with technology, socially liberal, engaged with the arts.[12] No doubt, comparable centers are being propagated throughout Europe, Asia, and Latin America. In the years ahead, however, this human enterprise will be complexified by three new players.

As we learn more about human biology—and particularly about the brain and about genes—we will discover those factors that either contribute to or diminish the likelihood of creative lives and creative activities. Perhaps certain genes control personalities or temperament that are receptive to innovation and accepting of turbulence; perhaps certain sites in the limbic system, or certain cross-cortical or inter-hemispheric connections, are more likely to be activated in individuals judged as "chronically creative" by the relevant fields. Such discoveries could simply be made and documented as "pure" scientific knowledge. It is far more likely, however, that those who value creativity will seek to cultivate—though hopefully not to breed!—human beings with those biological proclivities. We can be even more certain that those who seek totalitarian control will find ways to eliminate these creative outliers. Instead of burning books, future totalitarian leaders or their brutal henchmen will excise key brain centers or knock out telltale genes. What was once the province of science fiction may well become the realm of science fact.

New knowledge will continue to accrue as well in the domains of artificial intelligence and computer simulation of human intellect. Computer programs will be devised—indeed, programs have already been devised—that yield new works of visual art and music, new commercial designs, new scientific patterns and hypotheses. Those hooked on creative activity will also use computers as intellectual prosthetics—manipulating variables or accumulating massive amounts of data that would have been inconceivable in a precomputer age. Most innovations today—from the architectural designs of Frank Gehry to the decoding of genomes by the company Celera—would not be possible without powerful computers (though Gehry himself still works by hand). Again, there will be a struggle between those who yoke these new forms of intellect for positive ends, and those who use them for purposes of control or destruction.

Neuro-, geno-, and silicon technologies are value neutral. While glossy magazines like to sing the praises of these "new age" developments, computer scientist Bill Joy warns against the destructive potentials of nanotechnology, genetic engineering, and robotics.[13] I share his anxiety that a cloned toxic agent or a computer programmed to fire atomic warheads could wreak havoc on life as we know it. Needed today is a generous dollop of creativity in the human sphere—in particular, in the ways in which we human beings relate to one another personally, carry out our work, and fulfill our obligations as citizens. It is to these moral and ethical considerations that I now turn.

CHAPTER 5

The Respectful Mind

THE ORIGINAL BEAD GAME

AS FAR BACK as a hundred thousand years ago, predecessors of homo sapiens were already decorating themselves with colored beads. In the view of scholars, members of one humanoid group were distinguishing themselves from other groups through a conscious decision to beautify (beadify!) themselves in a prescribed manner.[1] We cannot know for sure whether such decoration was carried out exclusively or primarily for a group-marking purpose; nor whether our ancestors were already conversing with one another in some kind of language or protolanguage; nor how such marking related to other early forms of symbolization, ranging from funerary rites to cave paintings of animals. It does seem clear that the application of marks that differentiate groups from one another is an important, enduring characteristic of our species.

Anthropologists and archaeologists have studied group membership from various angles. Many human artifacts—such as masks, totem poles, and shields—are decorated with distinctive signs. Kinship patterns are often exogamous: men select partners from neighboring tribes, with names of offspring and patterns of residence as enduring, consequential concerns. The exchange of gifts between groups marks ceremonial occasions. But such identifying features are scarcely restricted to peaceful or celebratory situations. Tribal groups often engage in ritual warfare, armed combat proceeding until a specified number of individuals has been slain on one side or the other. In recent times, the ritualistic aspects of conflicts have atrophied: that's what's meant by chilling phrases like *total war, world war, global conflict,* or *mutually assured destruction.*

Humans exhibit a deep-seated tendency to create groups, to provide distinctive marks for these collectivities, and to adopt clearly positive or clearly hostile attitudes toward neighboring and more distant cohorts. Think soccer teams! Think rivalry among Internet service providers! Relationships range from long-lasting friendships to enduring rivalry to mortal enmity. The anthropologist Claude Lévi-Strauss considered the dichotomization of social relationships as a chief characteristic of human beings. In his terse account, social life consists of exchanges between cultural groups of three entities: words, goods, and women.

COMPETING EXPLANATIONS OF THE RELATIONS BETWEEN GROUPS

You can foreshadow the explanatory framework that you favor by examining your own reaction to the state of affairs I've just sketched. Fifty years ago, in the wake of Nazi pseudoscientific theories of race, observers were loath to adopt biologically based explanations of human behaviors. And so, the tendency to break into groups and thereby to organize social life was seen as a cultural legacy, one that could be voluntarily altered. Nowadays, our explanatory scaffolding tilts toward biology. Scholars emphasize analogies across the order of primates; researchers search for evidence that parts of the brain, or even specific genes, are associated with the recognition of group differences and the delineation of the congenial or hostile relations that may prevail between the groups.

The insights from sociobiology and evolutionary psychology are genuine. No doubt human beings have deeply entrenched inclinations to delineate groups, to identify with and value members of their own group, and to adopt a cautious if not antagonistic tone to other comparable groups, however defined and constituted. But such biologically accented explanations have limitations. To begin with, they do not account for the contours, breadth, or flexibility of such ingroup-outgroup distinctions. (Consider the changing relations between Britain and France over the decades and over the centuries.) Second, since human beings exhibit both aggressive/ antagonistic *and* altruistic/affiliative tendencies, virtually any stance toward another group can be retroactively rationalized. Finally, even if biological bases can be found for dichotomization, stereotypy, or prejudice, human beings in every generation must attempt to deal with these proclivities and, when possible, to mute or overcome them. (Your reaction to the term *cosmopolitan* is a litmus test of your own thoughts about this issue.) Indeed, the peaceful trends of recent years in places like Northern Ireland and South Africa would be inexplicable were a once hostile relationship between groups—Catholic versus Protestant, colored versus white—truly implacable.

THE PRESENT ERA AS DIFFERENT

With the devising of mass weaponry, nuclear weapons chief among them, the relationship between human groups has crossed a Rubicon. In the past, when the built-in strictures that regulate ritualized warfare failed to operate, the worst outcome was the annihilation of a hostile group. Though the word may be new, the concept of *genocide* is as old as the Bible and as recent as events in the Sudan, Rwanda, and the former Yugoslavia. Nowadays, warfare knows no limits. In less than a century we have had two conflicts that encompassed much of the globe. And we possess nuclear, biological, and chemical weapons that can readily cross territorial boundaries and that could—in the extreme—render the world uninhabitable. It is remarkable that such weapons have so far been used only in limited contexts; it requires unalloyed optimism to believe that world-threatening conflagrations will not occur within the lifetimes of readers of this sentence.

Outlawing war and weapons is a noble idea, but one that seems unlikely to be realized. Groups do not trust one another to carry through on such commitments, and perhaps they are wise to be wary of adversaries bearing such promissory notes. (When I was young, a solitary name—*Munich*—signaled a skepticism about a leader's promise to maintain the peace.) Competition of various sorts—ranging from commercial to athletic—may serve as a substitute form of combat for some individuals and some groups; but the notion that countries boasting competitive soccer teams or a ribbon of McDonald's restaurants will accordingly refrain from war is naive. As far as I can see, short of peace pills or widespread extirpation of those brain nuclei or genes that support aggressive behaviors, the only possible avenue to progress lies in education, broadly conceived.

A REASONABLE GOAL: RESPECT FOR OTHERS

In a world composed of a few hundred nations, thousands of groups speaking thousands of languages, and more than 6 billion inhabitants, what is a reasonable goal? Clearly, we can no longer simply draw a curtain or build a wall that isolates groups from one another indefinitely. We homo sapiens must somehow learn how to inhabit neighboring places—and the same planet—without hating one another, without lusting to injure or kill one another, without acting on xenophobic inclinations even if our own group might emerge triumphant in the short run. Often the desideratum *tolerance* is invoked, and it may be the case that it is all that we can aspire to. Wordsmiths of a more optimistic temperament opt for romantic language; on the eve of World War II, poet W. H. Auden declared, "We must love one another or die."[2]

I prefer the concept of respect. Rather than ignoring differences, being inflamed by them, or seeking to annihilate them through love or hate, I call on human beings to accept the differences, learn to live with them, and value those who belong to other cohorts.

DEVELOPMENTAL MILESTONES

Even in the opening year of life, we can discern a basis for the respect of others. Infants in a nursery see or hear the distress of another infant; they signal their awareness by whimpering or crying themselves. Psychologists construe these behaviors as an incipient sense of self (as compared to other), and as the emergence of an empathic response. Toddlers, slightly older, become proactive when confronting the distress of another; they will soothe a toddler who seems sad—giving her a toy, asking her to join in a game.

Alas, less docile responses are also detectable. Toddlers will grab toys from one another, taunt one another, fight with one another, exclude individuals ("you're a baby") or groups ("this corner is only for boys") from valued activities. In pathological cases, youngsters will go beyond mere self-centeredness and actively seek to injure someone else. The capacity to distinguish groups from one another is also manifest well before the start of formal schooling: youngsters age three or four can make consequential distinctions between individuals or groups in terms of skin color, gender, language, dress

style, place of residence, and perhaps even ethnicity. Indeed, even in
the first months of life, infants look preferentially at faces of their
own race—but not, instructively, when they live in a culture which
features large numbers of individuals of different skin colors.[3]

Detection of differences is the raw material—part of human
cognition, useful in many ways, impossible to stem in any case. But
how those differences are labeled and interpreted is a cultural phenomenon. Young children identify with—and want to emulate—
individuals who are seen as bigger, older, and/or more powerful.
How these admired role models relate to membership in different
groups becomes crucial. If white and black adults mix readily and
comfortably, the salience of this color distinction is reduced. If
adults speak a number of languages and move readily from one pa-
tois to another, this facility in communication underscores the connections among linguistic groups. When my daughter Kerith came
home from preschool, she asked, "Is Mrs. Chase black?" Clearly, she
had heard this term but was uncertain to what it referred. When
famed preschool teacher Vivian Paley admonishes her young charges
that "you can't say 'you can't play,'" she is laying down a precept that
enlarges a sense of belonging and imposes a penalty on those who
would be divisive.[4]

By the age of five, at the latest, the lines for friendship or hostil-
ity, group inclusion or group exclusion, love or hatred, have already
been drawn. Youngsters are cognizant of group identities and delin-
eations. Based on what they observe, they have already begun to
adapt stances toward the groups to which they belong, the groups
from which they feel excluded, and/or the groups to which they
do not wish to belong. It matters enormously to the development
of social attitudes and degree of comfort whether a young person
has been raised in the apartheid South Africa of the 1950s or the
integrated South Africa of the present era.

An important issue is whether young people attach moral significance to group membership: in other words, is group A simply

different from group B—or is group A better (or worse) than group B? Even five-year-olds have a sense of the moral domain as a domain apart: they can distinguish practices that are moral (it is simply wrong to steal or to harm another) from practices that are merely conventional (in some countries people drive on the left side of the road). And they may also share some moral intuitions—for example, that goods should be distributed equally among members of a group. But whether young persons will invest group differences *per se* with moral force ("those with my skin color are better than those of a different skin color") cannot be foretold. One of the factors that swayed the Supreme Court in the famous *Brown v. Board of Education* case of 1954 was the demonstration by psychologists that, given a choice, many black children preferred to play with white dolls. The attitudes and practices of the surrounding community proved crucial in that determination.

Ideally, the responsibility of engendering respect among different groups, and displaying that respect publicly, should be distributed across the society. Parents, neighbors, political leaders, religious leaders, the popular media, and the range of community organizations should all exhibit such respect. More, they should reward those who exhibit respect and isolate or otherwise penalize those who fail to show respect—in the current parlance, those who "dis" others. But we cannot count on a prevalence of such ideal role models. Much more likely, the growing person encounters a whole range of models, some admirable perhaps, but many others mixed or even quite hostile. If you doubt this, just flip cable channels on the nearest television set or scan the dial on talk radio.

Often a dissociation emerges between public expression of tolerance and subtler signs of snobbishness, prejudice, or frank exclusion. Psychologist Yarrow Dunham and his colleagues have shown that, by the years of middle childhood, youngsters deny that they are prejudiced.[5] Yet, placed in an experimental paradigm where reaction times to stimuli signal underlying prejudices, these same youngsters reveal that they favor their own group and groups of high status, while disdaining members of other groups and particularly those that have less prestige. (To be specific: subjects respond more quickly when positive labels are attached to groups that they respect, and negative labels are attached to groups that they disdain.) The same dissociation between overt tolerance and covert prejudice has been observed among American youngsters and Japanese youngsters. By the time that young persons become adolescents or young adults, their attitude toward others is pretty well fixed; barring extremely unusual circumstances, one's stance toward other groups is unlikely to change fundamentally. It is not pleasant to learn of the enduring nature of prejudice and prejudices; yet, unless we recognize and acknowledge this pervasive tendency, we are unlikely to be able to surmount it.

A RESPECTFUL MILIEU AND FALSE VARIANTS THEREOF

The task for educators becomes clear: if we are to fashion persons who respect differences, we need to provide models and offer lessons that encourage such a sympathetic stance. Such modeling is especially crucial when the power relationships between individuals or groups appear to be asymmetrical.[6] Models set by teachers constitute a crucial starting point. Students take keen note of how teachers treat one another, how they treat other adults, and how they treat students—particularly those who come from a nonmajority group (e.g., a religious minority or a cohort of recently arrived immigrants). The literary, graphic, and experiential curricula selected by teachers; the way that these curricula materials are treated; and, perhaps especially, the materials that are *not* selected or are prematurely dismissed exert a powerful effect. Just consider the difference between a white-majority classroom that reads and discusses with sympathy books by and about black individuals, and a comparable classroom in which works by black authors are scorned or not encountered at all. Famed novelist Saul Bellow did not help the cause of intercultural respect when he taunted, "Who is the Tolstoy of the Tutus, who is the Zola of the Zulus?"[7]

Turning to specific disciplines, I do not believe that science and mathematics ought to be inflected as a means of honoring group differences. As universal languages, these ought to be construed and taught similarly around the globe. When it comes to history, the arts, and the humanities, however, clear choices need to be made. The history of a country turns out to be quite different, depending on whether it is formulated primarily in terms of political, economic, social, or cultural considerations. A historical treatment of the Spanish Civil War can aim for a neutral stance or display sympathy to the Loyalist or the Fascist cause. I believe that these human-inflected topics should be taught in light of a range of perspectives. This does not mean, however, that all sides in a dispute are worthy of respect. There may have been valid reasons for German citizens to support the Nazis in depression-wracked Germany of 1930; there are no valid reasons to defend the Nazis' bellicose stance by the end of the decade, let alone the decision by Hitler and his henchmen to eliminate Jews and other "undesirable" or "impure" elements.

Messages of respect or disrespect, tolerance or intolerance, are signaled throughout a society. Many lessons are drawn from the presence or absence of members of different groups in athletics, the media, the political arena; and even more inferences are drawn in light of the roles assumed by such group members and the ways in which majority or elite interests in the society treat less powerful individuals and groups. A corporation can boast a scorecard of 20 percent employment of African American workers. But the visitor or the recent hire will soon notice whether the blacks are receptionists or managers, whether those in the boardroom are serving or being served, which groups are regularly featured in ads or media presentations and which are consigned to the sidelines or featured only for select audiences.

Indeed, I would go so far as to say that the genuine measures of respect are detectable every day, when, so to speak, no one is actively looking. It is elementary for a politician—be it a mayor, a senator, even a president—to say that he (or she) loves all human beings; it is easy to place minorities in visible positions and to be photographed with them. The skeptical observer notes who are the politician's regular advisers, who is dispatched to high-stake (as opposed to ceremonial) meetings, with whom the politician spends quality time, jokes, plays golf, and shares confidence and moments of intimacy.

What are the signs of false respect or pseudorespect? Alas, signs of false respect abound. A common variety that has recently acquired its own vivid label is the tendency to kiss up and to kick down. All too many individuals in positions of power have attained their status, in part, because of their abilities to flatter and serve those who already occupy positions of authority. But when these same individuals are seen to ignore, beat up on, or disparage those with lesser influence, they reveal their lack of genuine respect for others.

I've had the opportunity to observe false respect over the years. On any number of occasions, I have formed a positive view of another person (let's call him Rex)—one who acts toward me in a friendly and considerate manner. But, then, in speaking to third parties, I have heard quite unfavorable reports about Rex. Examination reveals a persistent pattern. Rex and I have been at the same level in an organization, or I have been Rex's supervisor, or Rex has wanted something from me, like a favorable job recommendation. In contrast, the persons who complain about Rex are ones who are not in a position to help Rex, or ones who in fact are dependent on him. I recall cases where Rex comes to assume a higher status with reference to me and thereupon begins to behave in a much less considerate manner. This "kiss-up, kick-down" scenario has taught me that Rex is perfectly capable of behaving in a respectful manner when he has something to gain from it. In that sense, he may be even more deplorable than a person who displays equal disrespect across the status hierarchy.

An analogous pattern is observed in individuals who know how to display respect in public settings, but who revert to stereotypical jokes or worse when the spotlight has been removed. Here the respect emerges as time- and situation-specific, rather than as an assumption that governs all human relations.

And then there is *political correctness*—now a derogatory or derisive term. When so used, *political correctness* refers to the practice of speaking and acting positively toward a certain group, just because that group has in the past been subjected to mistreatment, and in decrying anyone who might say anything critical about that group. In turn, *political incorrectness* refers to the practice of undercutting political correctness—that is, deliberately saying or doing something critical of the targeted group or those who would shield it from criticism.

Determining whether an instance of so-called political correctness involves respect is not easy. When one acts in the same way toward all members of a group, simply by virtue of their group membership and without an effort to distinguish among members, I would not consider that to be a sign of respect. But if one's behavior toward individuals reflects a genuine effort to help and understand each person, then I would consider that pattern to be respectful. Political incorrectness, on the other hand, involves disrespect both toward the politically correct and toward those groups whose lots the politically correct are seeking to improve.

A truly respectful individual offers the benefit of the doubt to all human beings. As much as possible, she avoids thinking in group terms. She reserves censure for those who truly deserve it. She remains open to the possibility that her judgment may have been wrong. And she is on the alert for a change in behavior that will in turn reinstate a feeling of respect toward that other individual.

In my view, respect should not entail a complete suspension of judgment. When a person consistently acts disrespectfully toward others, that person should be called to account. And should disrespect persist, and deteriorate into frankly antisocial behavior, that person should be ostracized from society. (On rare occasions, an entire group may forfeit its right to be respected.) Mahatma Gandhi kept reaching out to Hitler; the Indian leader wrote a letter to Hitler, addressed "Dear friend," calling on him to change his tactics and promising him forgiveness in return.[8] In turn, Hitler remarked, "Shoot Gandhi, and if that does not suffice to reduce them to submission, shoot a dozen leading members of Congress [Gandhi's political party]."[9] When unconditional respect inadvertently encourages antihuman responses, it is counterproductive.

THE VALUE OF RESPECTFULNESS

One can have excellent scientific, mathematical, and technical education in an environment that is extremely intolerant. Precisely this situation often materializes in regimes that are fundamentalist in religious temper or totalitarian in political terms. If one wishes to raise individuals who are respectful of differences across groups, a special burden is accordingly placed on education in the social sciences, the human sciences, the arts and literature. Put bluntly, such education cannot bypass issues of respect under the rubric of "pure" disciplinary study. Rather, it is necessary to confront directly the value of respect, the costs of respect, and the infinitely greater costs of disrespect (in the long run).

During the early years of school, such issues are best approached through experiences in which members of different groups work together on common projects, come to know one another firsthand, deal with differences in an amicable manner, and discover that a perspective may be different without being deficient. Additionally, it is important to read books, see movies, and engage in games and simulations where respectful relations between individuals and groups are modeled and fostered. Lest the role of milieu seem unimportant, let me mention a slogan that I noted in a museum re-creation of a German classroom of 1912. Believe it or not, a large poster on the wall bore the legend (in German) "One must hate the neighbors." Is it any wonder that a world war broke out two years later, with Germany on one side, and several of her neighbors on the opposing Allied side?

While they are easy to poke fun at, the current efforts in American education to give equal time to a range of religious holidays, and to prototypical heroes from different groups, are well motivated. These efforts carry special meaning for members of minorities who may feel that they have been invisible in the power structure of their society. Yet, to the extent that these ecumenical efforts are seen as politically correct window dressing, or are not borne out by behaviors on view each day, they may prove useless or even counterproductive. Members of the majority group see them as idle gestures, devoid of genuine meaning; members of minority groups see them as patronizing efforts to buy off possible critiques. Such tensions are prevalent in western European countries that, in recent decades, have absorbed millions of immigrants from Africa, Asia, and the poorer regions of Europe. The stability and psychological health of "old Europe" will be determined by whether immigrants are ignored, patronized, or granted a genuine place in their new land. Terrorism has many causes, but surely a feeling of profound alienation in one's current abode is chief among them.

As one passes through the years of middle childhood and enters adolescence, a significant amount of time should be spent dealing explicitly with issues of group membership and group conflict. At this time it is appropriate to offer courses such as Facing History and Ourselves. This well-known offering in the American curriculum typically begins with the Holocaust of the Second World War and proceeds to encompass instances of racial and ethnic conflict from various corners of the globe. Whether reading works of literature, dissecting the history or the political system of various nations, examining the artistic productions of a region, or discussing current events, students should be brought face-to-face with how groups have related to one another in the past and how they might productively connect in the future.

Let me respond to two possible objections. First of all, I can by no means guarantee that greater tolerance will follow on such open discussion. Indeed, the opposite result may prevail initially, as students (often reflecting what they have heard at home or on the playground or via the mass media) give voice to deep reservations about groups different from their own. Airing these views is a necessary, though often uncomfortable, aspect of learning. Jewish people do not enjoy hearing the prejudices of gentiles (nor do gentiles welcome the prejudice of Jews); but unless these caricatures are voiced, and their merits and distortions are openly addressed, such misconceptions will simply fester beneath the surface, ripe for exploitation by a demagogue.

Second, I do not mean to suggest that the disciplines of history or literature or economics should be sacrificed to the study of group relations. No doubt, aspects of these disciplines can and should be taught with "neutral" materials; some facets of historical dating or microeconomics are as universal as mathematics or biology. But it is equally important that educators include in their disciplinary instruction clear-cut instances where group relations have been key or even determining factors—as so often happens in human affairs.

So far, I have discussed respect chiefly in the context of the values and milieus of school. But of course, respect is equally important at the workplace and in civil society. It is evident that organizations and communities work more effectively when the individuals within them seek to understand one another (despite their differences), to help one another, and to work together for common goals. Examples of positive leadership are crucial here, and clear penalties for disrespect—including ostracism or dismissal—are important as well. Less clearly understood is that respect within an organization is difficult to maintain when those outside the organization are deemed enemies. After all, one's competitors are human as well; one might well have ended up at the rival organization; and after the next merger or takeover, one might even be absorbed into the bowels of the former rival. The story is told of how, in an effort to motivate his football team, the Harvard coach once strangled a bulldog—the mascot of rival Yale. I hope that this story is apocryphal.

Some important insights have emerged from studies of teams at work. In studies of teams involved in cardiac surgery, Amy Edmondson and colleagues have documented that successful teamwork depends more on the management skills than on the technical expertise of their leaders.[10] Members of the teams respond favorably when their suggestions are taken seriously and when reflections on a procedure occur in a collegial manner. Writing in a similar vein, David Garvin and Michael Roberts counsel leaders to construe decision making as a process rather than an event.[11] Members of a group should be encouraged to ask questions of one another, to weigh the pros and cons of alternatives, to advocate positions other than their own; such an approach militates against hierarchy and promotes buy-in once a decision has been made.

Based on his own experiences as founder and executive of Xerox's Palo Alto Research Center (known familiarly as PARC), John Seely Brown speaks directly about the respectful organization.[12] He sought to understand why brilliant technological innovations were often launched at PARC and yet regularly spurned by the larger Xerox culture—thus enriching the coffers of rival Apple Computer rather than sponsoring Xerox Corporation. Brown concludes that the innovators at PARC neither understood nor respected the engineers and managers at Xerox, and the lack of empathy extended equally in the other direction. This dispiriting picture began to change when members of each distinctive culture made genuine efforts to understand, rather than to stereotype, the other. The engineers and marketers took the risk of entering the culture of PARC, and the designers and inventors wore the hats of those charged with meeting the bottom line at the parent company: the result was enhanced mutual respect and, ultimately, greater success for the larger Xerox entity.

On occasion, the value of disrespect has been lauded. In a deliberately provocative essay, Rodney Kramer defends those executives who play tough with their employees, who rule by insult and intimidation rather than by reason and reassurance.[13] Kramer suggests that such tactics are at a particular premium when rapid change is necessary in an organization that has been somnolent. He argues, further, that employees often come to value such bullying tactics: the words and deeds of the intimidator clear the air, get rid of deadwood, and encourage these same employees to develop thicker skins. I don't doubt that such tactics can be effective in the short run and that they may even help the occasional turnaround. But should they become the norm, they destroy the fabric of an organization. In the long run, rule by fist, fiat, fear, and fury is destined to fail. Moreover, it is far easier to call for such a stance when one is an outsider than when is housed (more precisely: trapped) within the stressed organization—be it a medical team struggling to save lives or an embattled corporation staving off bankruptcy.

Inculcation of respect is easiest to achieve in the early years of life. But if I may use myself as an example, it is never too late. Twice in recent years, I had an initial nonrespectful response to a situation. In both cases, spurred in part by my work on this book, I changed my mind.

When I first heard that an official in France had decided to bar Muslim girls and women from wearing veils and other religious garb to school, I sympathized with the ruling. After all, French schools have been determinedly secular for two centuries and those in attendance should respect that nonreligious commitment. But then, weighing the costs to the women of the deprivation of an important part of their religion, and realizing that the veils did not really impinge on anyone else's liberties, I concluded that respect should trump a longstanding norm.

Similarly, when I first heard about the decision of Danish newspapers to publish cartoons that were critical of Muslim leaders and practices, I felt that freedom of speech ought to prevail. But when I detected the degree of hurt felt by Muslim persons all over the world and—eventually—learned of the violence that ensued, I reconsidered my initial leanings. Cartoons are a particularly vicious form of ridicule, and especially insulting to those who are unfamiliar with that idiom. While artists should be allowed to draw what they like, and newspaper editorialists should feel free to criticize any and all institutions, the damage done by publication of the cartoons seems excessive and unnecessary. Neither the artists nor the free press would have suffered unduly if the critiques had been expressed in words, rather than pictures. For this reason, I would continue to defend the right of Salman Rushdie to publish *The Satanic Verses*, and of course condemn those who issued a fatwa on him.

I cite these examples not to insist that respect should always trump other virtues, nor to indicate that my changes of heart were necessarily correct. Rather, in the complex global terrain in which we now live, we should, whenever possible, give priority to respect for those with different backgrounds and beliefs—and hope that they will return the favor.

RESPECT AGAINST THE ODDS

The many flavors of respect can be nurtured in a myriad of ways. Those of a philosophical disposition approach this realm through discussion of morality, ethics, human rights, and obligations. A happy outcome of such an approach is a view of all humans as part of a single community. (Sometimes, such universality extends to all animals or even to the entire sacrosanct universe of living and non-living entities.) Some favor experiential modes of interaction. Such individuals crave play, employment, or voluntarism with a variety of individuals; the hope is that more nuanced views will emerge on the ground. School programs that inculcate philanthropic tendencies are promising. In a New York City–based program called Common Cents, youngsters collect pennies from the community and then decide as a group how to allocate these financial resources. Additionally, individuals with a potential for leadership should be guided to use their skills to promote positive, inclusive membership and missions. Individuals with an entrepreneurial bent should be encouraged to build organizations that serve the common good, rather than more selfish ends, and that recruit and promote across the demographic spectrum. How preferable it is for young people to join together to build homes or offer free concerts for the poor, rather than to go on drunken binges in the streets or smoke pot in their neighbor's basement. Adolescents have potentials for leadership, or for enterprise, that can be marshaled for diverse ends; it is up to their elders—parents, educators, community leaders, slightly older and more mature peers—to influence how these potentials are mobilized.

In this context, it is instructive—and shocking—to learn about the attendees at the Berlin Wannsee Conference of January 1942, where the decision to undertake the "final solution" was implemented. Of the fourteen individuals in attendance, all men, eight of them had advanced degrees from Central European universities. Clearly, years of schooling are no guarantor of a respectful mind.

No single formula reliably yields individuals who are respectful of others. Particularly valuable evidence comes from studies of rescuers—inhabitants of Nazi-occupied Europe who, at considerable risk to themselves, elected to hide Jews or other hunted individuals. According to Samuel Oliner, rescuers appeared quite ordinary on the surface; they resembled many others who were bystanders and even some who actively aided the Gestapo.[14] Closer study revealed telltale differences. Rescuers were marked by a childhood during which their parents avoided physical punishment, opting instead for lucid explanations of rules and practices. The rescuers stood out from their fellow citizens in the strong values—often but not invariably religious—that they absorbed from their parents; a constructive and optimistic stance that they assumed toward life; feelings of connectedness to others, even those from a different group; and above all, an intuitive (indeed instinctive) reaction that what was being done to the innocent was wrong and that they themselves were capable agents who ought to (indeed, who must) take corrective action.

In recent years, intriguing efforts have been undertaken by individuals to help bring about rapprochement between groups that have long been alienated from one another. Some have sought to build bridges through joint participation in musical activities. Working with the late Edward Said, a Palestinian American writer, Daniel Barenboim, a Jewish pianist and conductor with multiple geographic roots, set up the West-Eastern Divan Workshop. This enterprise features an orchestra consisting of young Israeli and young Arab musicians. Summering together in the relatively neutral terrain of western Europe, these young musicians work together on pieces from the classical (mostly European) repertoire. In the evenings they hold open discussions in which they discuss sensitive political and cultural issues with individuals from the "other" group; often this encounter is the first time that a young Israeli or Palestinian has actually spoken with persons who had hitherto represented the enemy.

The joint activities of making music together by day and talking through difficult issues in the evening have the effect of bringing members of the two groups closer together. As explained by

Barenboim and Said, "They were trying to do something together, something about which they both cared, about which they were both passionate . . . [T]he transformation of these kids from one thing to another was basically unstoppable . . . [I]n cultural matters, if we foster this kind of contact, it can only help people feel nearer to each other and this is all."[15]

To be sure, an orchestra involving several dozen young Middle Eastern youth cannot solve the problems of an area that has been wracked with conflict for centuries. Moreover, both creators of this orchestra were themselves controversial individuals, with no small potential for polarizing supporters and critics. (It is doubtful that they could have accomplished what they did without skirting controversy.) As Barenboim commented, "A person who is determined to do something constructive with his life needs to come to terms with the fact that not everyone is going to love him."[16] Still, the very act of creating an orchestra and a series of politically oriented workshops is a courageous, praiseworthy one; like the Ping-Pong diplomacy that helped bring about the Sino-American thaw in the early 1970s, an artistic rapprochement may help eventually bring about political reconciliation. Indeed, during the very week in 2005 that the Gaza Strip was being returned to the Palestinians, the youth orchestra performed in the city of Ramallah. And in the summer of 2006, when Israel and the Lebanese Hezbollah were shelling one another, the orchestra performed in thirteen cities. Barenboim commented, "[T]his is a very small reply to the terrible horrors of war."[17]

Inspired by this initiative, but taking a somewhat different tack, renowned cellist Yo-Yo Ma launched the Silk Road Project in 1998. The artistic purpose of the project is to bring to wider attention the music of the many lands that constituted the old Silk Road—a lengthy, intercontinental trade route that was traveled by thousands of merchants from the first millennium BC to the second millennium AD. In performing music from countries like Iran, Kazakhstan, Uzbekistan, Turkey, and China, using both composers and performers from those lands, Ma and his associates hope to be able to convey important lessons about humankind: that there is no purely original music though there are authentic artistic traditions; that all societies learn from one another historically and contemporaneously; and that joy and understanding can emanate from excellent performances of many musical traditions and hybrids.

As one born in France of Taiwanese parents, trained in anthropology, living in America but traveling the world continuously, Ma is eager to use the project as a way of underscoring the essential affinities between all human beings. The project "hopes to promote collaboration and a sense of community among musicians, audiences, and institutions who share a fascination with the kind of transcultural artistic imagination symbolized by the silk road."[18] Ambitious in its aim, the Silk Road Project is developing various kinds of educational aids; these are designed to help teachers and students learn about remote parts of the world, feel at ease with the inhabitants and artworks of those regions, and appreciate the evolution of cultures and the impact of an ancient geographic entity on the world of today.

These two projects in music seek to bring about better understanding and heightened mutual respect through means that are primarily nonverbal. What about situations where horrendous criminal acts have been perpetrated primarily by a group in power against other, less powerful citizens?

Crucial clues come from commissions on truth and reconciliation that have been set up in recent years in South Africa and two dozen other societies as well. Such commissions grow out of a twin realization. On the one hand, brutal, unforgivable acts have been committed against members of a group, often simply on the basis of accidental factors: who their biological parents were, and where they happened to grow up. (*Ethnic cleansing* is the euphemism; all too often, genocide is the reality.) On the other hand, if the ambient society is to endure in the longer run, it is crucial for members of both groups—the victims but also the victimizers—to be able to move on.[19]

Following the saintly examples of Mahatma Gandhi and Nelson Mandela, members of the injured parties must abjure the reflexive weapons of retaliation, the "eye for an eye" philosophy that over the centuries has fueled an unending cycle of violence. Instead, the victims offer the gift of reconciliation to those individuals who are willing to admit their actions, apologize for those actions, express contrition, and ask for forgiveness. Such forgiveness is not always possible, and it is hardly ever easy to grant. But it is at times possible for individuals to put the past behind them, at least to tolerate one another, and, in the happiest instance, to acquire a measure of mutual respect.

Over the decades, these commissions have evolved quite specific procedures from moving from hatred to tolerance and, ultimately, to respect. The procedures vary from commission to commission and from land to land, but certain themes recur. To begin with, the commissions are not legal or war tribunals: they do not seek to mete out justice. Rather, they are designed to bear witness to what happened, as specifically and comprehensively as possible. Initially, representatives of the commission collect copious background information. Then, often at public hearings, victims are invited to tell their stories in as much rich detail as they would like and can endure. Those who inflicted damage on the victims, or on the victims' relatives (who may have been murdered), are then asked to account for their own actions. In the best instance, the victimizers respond candidly, repent their transgressions, offer their apologies, and seek forgiveness: a sequence of acknowledgment, contrition, and forgiveness.[20] And in some instances, forgiveness is actually granted by the aggrieved parties.

Commissioners listen carefully to the proceedings. They offer support to the victims and embolden them to detail their stories; as legal scholar Martha Minow has pointed out, the paradigms are healing and mercy, not justice and disinterestedness.[21] The commissions also support the victimizers, to the extent that their participation seems well motivated and sincere. For contemporary as well as historical purposes, commissions aim to document what happened as fully as possible. In some cases, they actually make recommendations about what should be done in a specific case—they may, for example, grant amnesty or mandate reparations. But their broader mission is to accomplish their work in a timely fashion and then offer guidance about how the society can heal and move on—never forgetting the past, but not being engulfed and submerged by it. In some cases the aim is overtly political—to strengthen the new regime and to buoy an emerging but still fragile democracy. And indeed, it has sometimes proved possible for the society to heal, for formerly estranged persons and groups to bury their differences and work side by side—at first tolerating, then ultimately respecting one another.

In overcoming hatred, rivalry, the burdens of history, it is crucial to search for common ground. For individuals who inhabit the same land, there is the possibility that they can be united by common experiences or loves or aspirations of the future. Those who were members of warring parties in the former Yugoslavia may rediscover a shared love of the land, mutual friends, even old mutual enemies. Inhabitants of Northern Ireland and the Republic of Ireland may learn to overlook differences in history and religion and instead to prize a common cultural tradition, language, and kinship. Longtime presidential rivals John Adams and Thomas Jefferson were reconciled in old age by an acknowledgment of the common struggles in which they had engaged when the colonies were seeking independence and by pride in the republic that they had both been instrumental in creating. Daniel Barenboim and Edward Said befriended one another through their mutual love of music and their aspirations for reconciliation among Semitic peoples.

Respect for others should permeate one's life. Most of us spend most of our waking hours at work. In our final portrait, we turn to the kind of mind that individuals should display as they pursue their vocations and fulfill their roles as citizens.

CHAPTER **6**

The Ethical Mind

IN WHAT KIND OF A WORLD would we like to live if we knew neither our standing nor our resources in advance? Speaking for myself—but, I trust, not only for myself—I would like to live in a world characterized by "good work": work that is excellent, ethical, and engaging. For more than ten years, Mihaly Csikszentmihalyi, William Damon, and I have been exploring the nature of good work; in particular, we and our colleagues have sought to determine which factors contribute to good work, which militate against it, and how best to increase the incidence of good work. Because our findings illuminate the ethical mind, I shall describe them in some detail.

As the founding social scientists of the late nineteenth century well understood, work stands at the center of modern life. Émile Durkheim delineated the indispensable and convincingly argued role of the division of labor in complex societies; Max Weber described the religious foundation of a "vocation" that goes beyond perfunctory performance and reflects our heartfelt response to divine calling; Sigmund Freud identified love and work as *the* keys to a good life. Conveniently, the English word *good* captures three distinct facets of work. Work may be good in the sense of being *excellent* in quality—in our terms, it is highly disciplined. Such work may be good in the sense of being *responsible*—it regularly takes into account its implications for the wider community within which it is situated. And such work may be good in the sense of feeling good—it is *engaging* and meaningful, and provides sustenance even under challenging conditions. If education is preparation for life, it is in many ways the preparation for a life of work. Educators should prepare young persons for a life marked by good work; the workplace and the broader society should support and sustain such good work.

A broad and ambitious study needs a point of departure. We decided to focus on good work in the professions. We conceptualize a profession as a highly trained group of workers who perform an important service for society. In return for serving in an impartial manner and exercising prudent judgment under complex circumstances, professionals are accorded status and autonomy. In our study thus far, we have interviewed more than twelve hundred individuals. Most of them work in established professions like medicine, law, science, journalism, and education. Also included in our sample are individuals who work in spheres that are not strictly considered professions—theater, philanthropy, business, and social entrepreneurship. Some of these individuals are just entering professional life; others are in mid-career; still others are veterans who are no longer full-time workers but who serve as trustees, monitoring the health of the profession and intervening as appropriate to maintain that health. Through in-depth interviews of these respected workers, we have sought to determine their goals; the forces that facilitate or thwart progress toward those goals; the ways that they proceed under often difficult circumstances; the formative influences on their own development; and the direction in which their profession is headed.[1]

From one angle, it is easy to identify professionals. They have earned a license; they pursue extensive and often continuing education, attend lots of meetings with peers on- and off-site, and live comfortably if not ostentatiously. If they do not act according to recognized standards, they stand at risk of being disbarred from their professional guild. But it is important to underscore that being recognized as a member of a profession is not the same as acting like a professional. Many individuals designated as professionals and dressed in expensive suits do not act in a professional manner; they cut corners, pursue their own interests, fail to honor the central precepts and strictures of their calling. They are executing "compromised work." On the other hand, many individuals who are not so designated officially behave in an admirable, professional-like manner. They are skilled, responsible, engaged, themselves worthy of respect. (We all prefer hotels, hospitals, and high schools staffed by such self-proclaimed professionals.) In what follows, I focus on individuals who behave like professionals, irrespective of their training: committed individuals who embody an ethical orientation in their work.

While our own research has focused on the world of work, the ethical mind is not restricted to the workplace. I believe that the role of a citizen calls equally for an ethical orientation—a conviction that one's community should possess certain characteristics of which one is proud and a commitment personally to work toward the realization of the virtuous community. Indeed, while a specific individual might choose to focus on the workplace, or to devote energy to the surrounding community, the ultimate ethical stance encompasses both entities. These realms share the characteristic that the individual must be able to step back from daily life and to conceptualize the nature of work and the nature of community. He or she needs to consider such questions as: What does it mean to be a lawyer/physician/engineer/educator at the present time? What are my rights, obligations, and responsibilities? What does it mean to be a citizen of my community/my region/the planet? What do I owe others, and especially those who—through the circumstances of birth or bad luck—are less fortunate than I am?

So conceptualized, ethics involves a stance that is inherently more distanced than face-to-face relationships embodied in tolerance, respect, and other examples of personal morality. In the jargon of cognitive science, ethics involves an *abstract attitude*—the capacity to reflect explicitly on the ways in which one does, or does not, fulfill a certain role. Later, I'll say more about the relation between respect and ethics.

SUPPORTS FOR GOOD WORK

The attainment of an ethical mind is easier when one has been raised in a milieu where good work is the norm. Just as we can recognize cultures (like China) where disciplinary work has been cultivated, or societies (like California's Silicon Valley) where creativity has been prized, it is possible to identify sites that have been characterized by good work. My own favorite contemporary example is the picturesque northern Italian city of Reggio Emilia, a community that I have visited and studied for twenty-five years. From everything that I have observed over the years, Reggio Emilia works exceedingly well. The community is civilized, offers high-quality services to its citizens, and is replete with artistic performances and treasures. For the past several decades this community of somewhat more than a hundred thousand individuals has devoted unparalleled human and financial resources to the development of quality infant-toddler centers and preschools. In 1991, *Newsweek* magazine dubbed these Reggio institutions "the best pre-schools in the world."[2] When visitors inquire what happens to the graduates of these schools for the young, longtime residents issue this short but revealing answer: "Just look at our community." Recalling an old term from show business, this answer is a "showstopper."

Reggio Emilia did not achieve excellence in work and in the community by accident. It sits in a region of the globe where civil society has existed for centuries. Voluntary communal services and cultural groups can trace their beginnings to the medieval era.[3] But

Reggio Emilia would not have achieved distinction in education in the absence of committed individuals who, in the aftermath of the devastation wrought by World War II, banded together to create the kind of community in which they and their children could thrive. They asked, in effect, what kinds of citizens do we want to produce?

Taking a bit of poetic license, I say that these leaders on the ground combined—indeed, synthesized—two usually contrasting worldviews. On the one hand, they have adopted the heart of socialist ideology—a society in which property is not aggressively accumulated, many goods are shared, and each individual works to the utmost of his or her abilities. On the other hand, they function like a Catholic monastery or nunnery—men and women working tirelessly together with little material reward—for the betterment of the broader society. Residents of Reggio Emilia earn plaudits in ethics for being good workers and good citizens.[4]

Vertical Support

An ethical orientation begins at home. Whether or not they actually observe their parents on the job, children know that one or both of their parents work. They see whether their parents take pride in their work, how they speak of their supervisors and their colleagues, whether work is simply a resented or barely tolerated means of putting food on the table or also embodies intrinsic meaning and sustenance. Work also takes place at home. Children observe their parents as they make decisions about how to maintain the home, what to do about needed repairs or optional improvements. How adults approach play is also significant: children note whether adults like to play, whether they play fairly, whether they strive only to win or also find meaning and "flow" in the play itself, irrespective of whether one happens to win or lose. Strong religious values—embodied as well as preached—can serve as important catalysts. And children observe their parents as citizens: Do they read and talk about the community? Do they vote? Do they pay their taxes willingly? Do they devote thought to how they might improve the community? Do they roll up their sleeves and participate, or is their motivation chiefly selfish, their involvement chiefly rhetorical?

Adults outside the home also exert influence. Youngsters note the comportment of relatives, visitors, and the workers whom they encounter on the street and in the marketplace: children can and do mimic such people. (I will come later to the influences exerted by teachers.) A community like Reggio Emilia provides a powerful model of how adults can guide young persons in a proactive, positive direction.

Once youths begin to think about a career, they pay special attention to adults who are pursuing related work. Whether or not they are aware of it, these adults serve as vivid role models; they signal the beliefs and behaviors, the aspirations and the nightmares, of members of the profession. In regulated professions, specific individuals are often designated as mentors. Thus, graduate students may be assigned advisers, medical interns work with head residents or senior physicians, recently minted lawyers have the opportunities to clerk for judges or to assist senior partners. Often, a mutual selectivity occurs: mentor and mentee choose one another. Most young workers appreciate the opportunity to have a mentor, and those deprived of mentors voice their frustration. But it must be recognized that not all mentors approach the ideal; some reject their mentees, and a few provide negative models—in our terms, they inadvertently serve as "antimentors" or "tormentors."

A religious background can lay the foundation for quality work and thoughtful citizenship. Businesspersons nominated as good workers report that their religious values guide their daily practices. Scientists who consider themselves secular today often cite early religious training as important in developing their values and their favored patterns of behavior. In contrast, among journalists or artists, religion is only rarely invoked. Religion emerges as a possible con-

tributor to good work, but not an essential one; a strong and enduring ethical basis, however founded, is what matters.

Whether or not they pore over the daily newspaper, young persons cannot fail to be aware of the political context in which they
live. The behavior (and misbehavior) of the powerful is splashed
across the media and perennially gossiped about on the street. Young
people also note the stances assumed by their parents toward political, economic, and cultural happenings. They know—or at least
sense—whether their parents vote, for whom they vote, whether
political allegiances extend beyond self-interest. Equally, to the extent that elders feel estranged from, or contemptuous of, the political context of the community, such attitudes, too, are absorbed by
their progeny.

Horizontal Support

In contemporary society, peers and colleagues assume importance.
From an early age young persons hang out with those who are
roughly their own age. They are strongly influenced by the behaviors and beliefs of these individuals, and especially those who are
seen as somewhat more knowledgeable, prestigious, and/or powerful. I dispute psychologist Judith Rich Harris's claim that the influence of parents pales in comparison to that exerted by peers; she
mistakenly construes a situation that happens to characterize parts
of contemporary American society as a law of evolutionary psychology.[5] But I do concur with Harris that one of the most important functions assumed by parents is the determination of the peer
group; those parents who leave friendships totally to chance may be
placing their children at risk.

The quality of peers proves especially critical during adolescence. At that period of life, young persons are experimenting with
different life options. It matters enormously whether the young
person falls in with individuals who are devoted to community service, academic studies, or absorbing hobbies; or with individuals

who are engaged in aimless, antisocial, or frankly criminal activities. And while in many cases there is little doubt about where the young person will find her peer group, in other instances the pulls of contrasting cliques are manifest, and subtle factors determine in which direction the young person will ultimately veer.

Peers remain crucial as the aspiring professional goes to the workplace, as either an apprentice or a full-fledged employee. A powerful professional code (like the Hippocratic oath), impressive role models, and the candidate's own ethical sense can all be undermined by the dubious behaviors of one's close associates. In our study of select young workers, we found that all of them knew what good work was and nearly all aspired to it. But too many of them felt that good work was a luxury that they could not afford at this early state of their career. On their own accounts (which could have been accurate reports or hyperbolic projections), their peers were hell-bent on achieving success and would cut whatever corners were necessary. Our subjects were not willing to cede their own chances. And so, sometimes with embarrassment, sometimes with insolence, they declared that they, too, were going to do what it takes to make their mark—even if it involves pretending to verify the source of a news story, failing to carry out a necessary experimental control, or reinforcing a hated stereotype on the theatrical stage. Once they had "made it," then, of course, they would become exemplary good workers. Here they were confronting a classic ethical dilemma: can a praiseworthy end justify dubious means?[6]

The estrangement of young people from the political system, particularly in the United States, is well documented. Many do not vote; few see themselves as becoming involved in politics. This estrangement may or may not be equated with a lack of citizenship. More than half of American teenagers are involved in some form of community service; and at some colleges and universities, the figure swells to two-thirds of the student population or even higher. One hundred million Americans report that they do some voluntary work, most often for their churches. Yet, the same individuals who may personally give much of themselves to their community are often extremely cynical about the political scene, locally and beyond. By distancing themselves, they foreclose on the possibility that they could contribute to political change. One may be amused by the comedian turned political critic Jon Stewart, but his blistering critiques do not point the way toward positive action. Ralph Nader is closer to the mark when he comments, "Citizenship is not some part-time spasmodic affair. It's the long duty of a lifetime."[7]

Periodic Inoculations

Suppose that the early determinants of ethical behavior are well aligned. The young person beholds admirable role models at home. She surrounds herself—or is fortunate enough to be surrounded—with young persons who are well motivated and upright. She has a worthy mentor. And her associates on the first job play by the rules. Surely, she is well on the road to becoming a good worker.

And yet, there are no guarantees. All manner of factors—ranging from the offer of a highly lucrative but shady job to improper practices at work that are condoned by the boss—may cause the young worker to wander from the ethical path. All workers can benefit from periodic inoculations. In some cases, these inoculations will be positive "booster shots": exposure to individuals and experiences that remind them of what it means to be a good worker. When a middle-aged physician becomes acquainted with an individual who gives up her high-paying suburban practice to become an emergency worker in the inner city, this experience may serve as a prod to carry out *pro bono* work. Or when Aaron Feuerstein, owner of Massachusetts–based Malden Mills, keeps his workers on the payroll even after the mills have burned down, other owners are stimulated to go the extra mile for their employees. However, "antiviral" inoculations may also be needed when negative examples come to light. Consider the misdeeds of the young *New York Times* reporter Jayson Blair, who destroyed a promising career by making up some stories and plagiarizing others. While his behaviors were destructive both for himself and—at least temporarily—for his newspaper, they caused a healthy reexamination of mentoring practices and editing standards throughout the journalistic profession. To cite an even more famous example, when major accounting firm Arthur Andersen went bankrupt because of its misdeeds in the Enron scandal, both large and small auditing partnerships reexamined their practices.

By now, you, the reader, may well be thinking:"This all sounds well and good. We can all agree about the desirability of good work. But who judges what work is good and what work is not? Where's the yardstick, and who designs it? How much agreement would we find, say, among the three Jesses: Jesse Ventura, Jesse Helms, and Jesse Jackson? Or among Bill Clinton, Bill Frist, and Bill Buckley? And, to raise the ante: didn't the Nazis think that they were doing good work?"

I'd be the first to concede that there is no foolproof metric for assessing the quality of work. But I'm willing to put forth candidate markers. A good worker has a set of principles and values that she can state explicitly, or at least acknowledge upon questioning. The principles are consistent with one another, and they sum to a reasonably coherent whole. The worker keeps these principles in mind constantly; asks whether she is abiding by them; and takes corrective action when she has not. The worker is transparent—to the extent possible, she operates out in the open and does not hide what she is doing. (To the extent that secrecy appears necessary, it should be no more than can withstand critical scrutiny at a later date—for example, no wholesale classification of documents as secret.) Most important, the worker passes the hypocrisy test: she abides by the principles even when—or especially when—they go against her own self-interest.

Perhaps, indeed, there are no truly universal ethics: or to put it more precisely, the ways in which ethical principles are interpreted will inevitably differ across cultures and eras. Yet, these differences arise chiefly at the margins. All known societies embrace the virtues of truthfulness, integrity, loyalty, fairness; none explicitly endorse falsehood, dishonesty, disloyalty, gross inequity.

Some readers may also be raising another issue: "This talk about good work has a moralistic tone to it. You can't expect to achieve good work by preaching it or by manipulating others. Adam Smith—and Milton Friedman after him—had the right instinct. If we let people pursue their own self-interest, by allowing the processes of the marketplace to operate freely, positive moral and ethical consequences will follow."[8]

I am not one to question the power and benefits of the marketplace in any absolute sense—like many others, I have been a beneficiary thereof and I've observed its dividends in many corners of the world. But I do not believe for a minute that markets will inevitably yield benign or moral outcomes. They can be cruel and, anyway, are fundamentally amoral. Adam Smith actually had a quite nuanced view of markets; their morality presupposed on a certain kind of society, inhabited by actors who were able to take a long- rather than a short-term view. Moreover, when he moved from a singular focus on transactions, Smith issued strong strictures: "He is certainly not a good citizen who does not wish to promote, by every means of his power, the welfare of the whole society of his fellow citizens."[9] My position is well expressed by Jonathan Sacks, chief rabbi of Britain: "When everything that matters can be bought and sold, when commitments can be broken because they are no longer to our advantage, when shopping becomes salvation and advertising slogans become our litany, when our worth is measured by how much we earn and spend, then the market is destroying the very virtues on which in the long run it depends."[10]

THREATS TO AN ETHICAL ORIENTATION

From one perspective, the threats to an ethical orientation are simply the converse of the factors that engender good work. I can run through them readily. If at home one lacks parents or guardians who embody ethical behavior; if one's childhood peers are selfish, self-absorbed, or self-aggrandizing; if one has a malevolent mentor or none at all; if one's initial associates on the job are prone to cut corners; and if one lacks periodic inoculations of a positive sort or fails to draw object lessons from instances of compromised work, then the chances that one will exhibit good work are minimal.

But in this individual-centered account, I have left out a crucial ingredient: the quality of institutions. It is easier to carry out good work in the community of Reggio Emilia because the standards of the constituent institutions are manifestly high. It is easier to carry out good work in those corporations, professional partnerships, universities, hospitals, foundations, or not-for-profit organizations in which the leadership—and the followership—strive to be good workers; select as members those who show promise of carrying out, or of continuing to carry out, good work; and remove, with prejudice, those rotten apples who threaten to infect the rest of the barrel.

However, it is not sufficient for an institution to have featured ethical work in the past. As the example of Jayson Blair at the *New York Times* reminds us, high standards offer no insurance against unsavory workers who execute work of poor quality. Indeed, sometimes the very reputation for good work can inadvertently undermine an institution. Veterans erroneously assume that those all around them share the same values, and thus they do not carry out the due diligence that is necessary to ensure the continuation of good work. Writing of the *New York Times* in the wake of the Blair scandal, journalist Elizabeth Kolbert said that this "paper of record" cannot afford to "check up" on its employees; it has to assume that they are trustworthy.[11] Lurid tabloids are less likely to make such an assumption.

A reputation for ethical work can also blind members of an institution to changing conditions. The Boston-based law firm of Hill and Barlow took pride in its century-long reputation for excellent work. Yet, following a meeting of senior partners on December 7, 2002, the firm abruptly closed its doors. From the outside, it looked as if the closing was due primarily to the announced departure of an avaricious group of real estate lawyers, who could double or triple their yearly take-home pay by abandoning their long-time professional home and associates. But closer examination by my colleague Paula Marshall turned up a different picture.[12] For three decades, the members of this esteemed law firm paid insufficient attention to the changing financial landscape and client base. And when, in the late 1990s, the partners finally introduced a new governance system, the system proved dysfunctional. Individual lawyers may still have been practicing their craft at a high level—the first sense of *good*. But they were no longer being responsible to their colleagues and to their community, and many of them were no longer finding meaning in their work—the latter two, equally important senses of the word *good*. Had a significant number of partners monitored the changing conditions and put into place appropriate governance a decade or two earlier, Hill and Barlow's tradition of quality work in the law might still be in place. The vast amount of institutional knowledge, the admirable institutional culture, and the potential for continuing good work would not have disappeared in one fell swoop.

The biggest threats to ethical work are posed by broader trends in the society. For much of the twentieth century, public auditors were seen as independent professionals who attested to the validity of financial records of businesses, large and small. Yet at the start of the twenty-first century, a series of accounting scandals erupted in the United States and abroad. It turned out that not only those at Arthur Andersen but also professionals at other leading firms had been behaving in clearly nonprofessional ways: maintaining very close ties to the corporations that they were supposed to be auditing; overlooking clear violations of regulations; certifying records that they knew to be misleading at best, and often frankly illegal; erecting questionable tax shelters; routinely blurring the line between consulting and auditing; and sometimes even shuttling their employment back and forth between the corporation and accounting firm. These individuals may have been securing financial rewards and feelings of "flow" from their activities, but in no way were they performing as excellent or ethical professionals.[13]

Studies of the accounting profession reveal that the control mechanisms thought to be in place were no longer functioning. Auditors may have paid lip service to the standards of fair and impartial accounting, but they no longer took their allegiance to the profession seriously. Promises of enormous financial rewards seduced those who were prepared to overlook or even embrace dubious practices. New employees saw their superiors crossing lines, favoring those employees who followed suit, and discouraging, if not firing, those who might blow the whistle on malpractice. The lure of the market was manifest; in the absence of powerful personal values, professional values, and/or strong legal or regulatory sanctions, too many members of a once honored profession carried out work that was seriously compromised, if not patently illegal.

Of course, in the recent past, the most famous case of unethical behavior is that displayed in the 1990s by the energy trading giant Enron. As now chronicled in a variety of articles and books, and in a memorable book and movie, *The Smartest Guys in the Room*,[14] Enron portrayed itself as one kind of a business when the reality was quite different. To admiring investors and journalists, Enron was the corporation of the future: a group of brilliant traders and executives who had figured out the operation of the energy markets and were using their knowledge in the service of shareholders and the broader society. By 2000, Enron was the seventh-most-capitalized company in the United States, with an estimated book value of $80 billion. The words of CEO Kenneth Lay were inspiring: "Enron could choose to think of only today and focus on maximizing profits. Instead, it has chosen to set the standard for a new industry by designing the rules of the game to be played in the next millennium. In the end this will benefit customers, Enron shareholders, and Enron employees. Bring on the brave new world."[15] And yet more: "Enron's reputation finally depends on its people, on you and me. Let's keep that reputation high."[16]

In truth, the success of Enron was achieved largely through smoke and mirrors. Taking advantage of loosely formulated regulations and nonexistent consciences, the executives were able to project future profits that had no foundation in present realities. As the actual financial position of the company worsened, executives created shadow, complicitous off-the-balance-sheet companies that were beholden only to Enron; devised special-purpose vehicles that hid debt; sold energy that did not exist; and manipulated the energy system in California in ways that were extremely costly and injurious to the citizens of that state and to employees in associated corporations. In ascertaining what went wrong, there is plenty of blame to go around—blame that extended beyond Enron to include its long-term accountant Arthur Andersen and many high-reputation financial institutions that colluded with Enron in shady transactions.

Yet, in my view, at the core of the malady were the unprincipled values of the leading figures in the company—some of whom have since been sentenced to terms in prison. Alas, these miscreants found all too many co-conspirators in the ranks of the company, on the board of directors, and in the other brand-name organizations with which they did business. As is too often the case, the victims were hapless employees in the lower ranks who lost their jobs, their lifetime savings, their trust in others, and their self-respect.

AN EDUCATION CENTERED ON GOOD WORK

Until the third decade of life, young persons spend more time in school than in any other institution. They are in the presence of teachers more than in the company of parents; they are surrounded by schoolmates more than by siblings or children in the neighborhood. Formal educational institutions play a key role in determining whether an individual is proceeding on the road to good work and active citizenship.

Teachers serve as crucial models. They introduce young persons to a vital (if often underappreciated) profession. Children observe the behavior of teachers; their attitudes toward their jobs; their mode of interaction with their supervisors, peers, and aides; their treatment of students; and most important, their reactions to the questions, answers, and work products of their students. It's been said that students in law school form an enduring concept of an instructor by the way he or she deals with the first moments of genuine discomfort in the classroom. In an encouraging note, our own studies reveal that, except for friends and families, young persons place most trust in their own teachers. For their part, most pupils are engaged in their first work experiences. The work of school is to master the manifest curriculum—be it the basic literacies, the major disciplines, or (in the future envisioned here) the more ambitious and more elusive contours of synthesizing or creative thought. In most schools nowadays, the focus falls almost exclusively on the achievement of excellence in these scholastic activities.

Educators can smooth the road to an ethical mind by drawing attention to the other connotations of goodness. Students need to understand *why* they are learning what they are learning and *how* this knowledge can be put to constructive uses. As disciplined learners, it is our job to understand the world. But if we are to be ethical human beings, it is equally our job to use that understanding to improve the quality of life and living and to bear witness when that understanding (or misunderstanding) is being used in destructive ways. This is a reason why community service and other forms of giving are—or should be—an important part of the curriculum of any school. Perhaps paradoxically, when students see that knowledge can be put to constructive use, they are most likely to gain pleasure from schoolwork and to find it meaningful in itself—thereby achieving the other facets of goodness.

As noted, the capacity to conceptualize these matters depends on the ability of the young person to think abstractly about herself as a worker and as a citizen. From an early age, of course, young people are influenced by what they see around them, what is rewarded, what is written about, what is ignored or disparaged. They certainly can engage in acts that are moral or immoral. And they may well benefit from eavesdropping on adult conversation about ethical issues. But only as the years of adolescence approach do students become able to think schematically and analytically about the contours of the roles that they will one day adopt: What does it mean to be a worker of one sort or another? What does it mean to be a citizen with one kind of leaning as opposed to an other?

Unlike younger persons, adolescents can readily imagine different possibilities, try out and see what it is like to be a scrupulous or an unscrupulous lawyer, a dedicated or a self-centered citizen. No longer do they dress up as Mommy or Daddy—they envision themselves as a journalist or as a judge. This is why adolescents are most susceptible to idealistic or utopian visions, even as they are uniquely prey to a course of immoral acts just to see what it is like. Often this idealism becomes tempered, as they enter the real world and encounter pressures to compromise. But the "best workers" and the "best citizens" do not let the difficulty of the task keep them from putting forth their best efforts.

At this point, it is appropriate to return to an issue mentioned earlier: the relationship between respect and ethics. I intend no sharp divide, no gulf, between these two spheres of virtue. It is difficult to imagine an ethical person who does not respect others, and those young persons who evince genuine respect toward others are most likely to become ethical workers and responsible citizens.

And yet, it is misleading to collapse these spheres. Respect (or disrespect) for others begins in the earliest years of life, and it remains fundamentally an issue of how an individual thinks of and behaves toward those persons whom he or she encounters each day. The equation is:

$$\text{Person} \rightarrow \text{Other Persons}$$

Ethics involves an additional step of abstraction; it is an achievement of adolescence and the decades thereafter. Taking an ethical stance, a person thinks of himself as a member of a profession and asks how such persons should behave in fulfilling that role; or he thinks of himself as a citizen of a locale, region, or the world and asks how such persons should behave in fulfilling those roles. The equation, and how a role should be enacted in appropriate institutions or settings, is:

Person→Role

The philosopher Peter Singer captures the distinction well:

If we are looking for a purpose broader than our interests, something that will allow us to see our lives as possessing significance beyond the narrow confines of our own conscious states, one obvious solution is to take up the ethical point of view. The ethical point of view does . . . require us to go beyond a personal point of view to the standpoint of an impartial spectator. Thus looking at things ethically is a way of transcending our inward looking concerns and identifying ourselves with the most objective point of view possible—with, as Sidgwick puts it, "the point of view of the universe."[17]

Two examples can be helpful here, one personal and humble, the other exalted and of historical significance. I supported Lawrence Summers when he first became president of Harvard in July 2001. I admired his achievements, liked him personally, and respected the office that he held. In the next few years, however, I saw multiple instances in which he disrespected individuals and harmed the institution that I valued. At first, like many others, I sought to give Summers advice that might help him be a more effective president, but for whatever reason, that advice did not take. Early in 2005, I made the personally painful decision to oppose him publicly and to advise him privately to resign. In making this decision, I had to mute my own personal feelings for Summers and my respect for the office that he currently held. Instead, I asked myself an ethical question: as a longtime citizen of the Harvard community, what is the right thing for me to do? At the cost of some friendships and much personal anguish, I elected to follow what appeared to me to be the ethical path—in the phrase of Albert O. Hirschman, to "let voice trump loyalty."[18]

From early in his childhood, Abraham Lincoln was made very uncomfortable by slavery. He never had slaves himself, and he did not want there to be slaves anywhere in his country. During his campaigns for Senate and president, he took a public position that was critical of slavery, and he was strongly opposed by slaveholders and by others who were sympathetic to slavery or opposed to federal intervention in the affairs of a sovereign state. Many expected that, once in office, Lincoln would move swiftly to outlaw slavery and emancipate the slaves. But he did not. In fact, for several years, his focus was on the maintenance of the union, irrespective of the status of slaves. As he wrote to New York editor Horace Greeley, "I have here stated my purpose according to my view of official duty and I intend no modification of my oft-expressed personal wish that all men everywhere could be free."[19] Reflecting at greater length on his own situation, Lincoln wrote to Kentucky editor Albert Hodges:

> *I am naturally anti-slavery. If Slavery is not wrong, nothing is wrong. I cannot remember when I did not so think, and feel. And yet I have never understood that the Presidency conferred upon me an unrestricted right to act officially upon this judgment and feeling. It was in the oath I took that I would, to the best of my ability, preserve, protect, and defend the constitution of the United States. I could not take the office without taking the oath. Nor was it my view that I might take an oath to get power and break the oath by using the power.[20]*

In the terms of the present analysis, Lincoln elected to suspend his own personal respect for individuals of all races in order to fulfill his ethical place as the elected leader of a nation. Ultimately, of course, he concluded that his role as preserver of the union came to encompass emancipation of the slaves. In so doing he brought the realms of respect and ethics into closer alignment.

No magic formula guarantees an ethical mind. Our studies show that good work is most likely to come about when all the parties involved with a profession want the same thing. For example, in the late 1990s, geneticists in the United States had a relatively easy time pursuing good work because just about everyone sought the same dividends from that work—better health and longer life. In contrast, professionally grounded journalists and accountants had a difficult time pursuing good work. The journalist's desire to carry out careful objective reporting clashed with the society's hunger for sensationalism and the publisher's desire for ever greater profits, and the accountant's opportunity for securing financial rewards clashed with the credo of the profession and the shareholders' (and the society's) requirement of scrupulously accurate reporting.

Good work is also easier to carry out when the worker is wearing a single occupational hat and knows exactly what that hat does and does not entail. When physicians are trapped between serving their patients and satisfying the demands of their health maintenance organization, compromised work is far more likely to emerge. The biologist working each morning on government-funded research at the university must take care that he does not compromise the scientific canon of openness when he ventures each afternoon to the privately held biotech company—where he heads the board of scientific advisers and is a major holder of shares and stock options. Students can sense whether their teachers are presenting what they believe is important or are simply satisfying the latest directive from the superintendent, the state, or the nation. Overall it matters enormously whether the various interest groups with a stake in that work are in harmony or in conflict; and whether the particular role models are confident about the hat that they are wearing and resist donning hats that impose contradictory marching orders.

The course of good work is much more difficult to determine when the various parties are misaligned. Returning to my two examples, the goals and means of President Summers—however well intentioned—were increasingly misaligned with those of large parts of the Harvard faculty, and so the ethical course for faculty members was difficult to discern. By the same token, Lincoln oscillated for years about the status of slaves in his country until he finally concluded that the preservation of the union required the emancipation of the slaves. Nowadays, almost all agree that Lincoln did the right thing: but he paid with his life, and reverberations from his decision echo till this day.

In the wake of scandals at many workplaces, the call for ethics courses has been ubiquitous. Beyond question, those institutions charged with the education of individuals in business and the professions need to respond to this request. Like too many law schools, too many business schools have seen the training of managers as a purely technical matter and have been content to ignore ethical issues or to provide a single palliative course, often an elective during the final semester. The featuring of case studies of ethical and nonethical behavior, the infusion of ethics concerns across the curriculum, the provision of role models who behave ethically, and the sanctioning of those who do not are all important enterprises for any institution involved in the training of future members of the corporate world.

But the assumption of greater responsibility on the part of schools of business in no way exonerates the companies themselves. Employees listen to what their leaders say, and, even more carefully, they watch what their leaders do. The difference is palpable between James Burke, the CEO of Johnson & Johnson, who immediately recalled all Tylenol products during the scare of the 1980s, and the executives of Coca-Cola/Belgium in the 1990s or of Merck/USA in the early 2000s, who denied any problems with their respective products (sodas, drugs) until confronted by the screams of the media and the uneasiness of the general public.

The case of Lockheed Martin, as related by ethicist Daniel Terris, is instructive in this regard.[21] On the heels of corporate scandals in the 1970s, this company, like many others, set up an ethics and business conduct division. Initially quite humdrum, the division gained in appeal and effectiveness when it developed attractive business games, based on the cartoon character Dilbert; the company required all employees to spend at least an hour each year involved in ethics training. On the positive ledger, this intervention raised the consciousness of employees about ethical issues at the workplace and may well have burnished their personal integrity. But as Terris indicates, the ethics program that he studied falls far short of confronting key issues of company policy and strategy. It does not touch on employment practices, fairness in the workplace, executive compensation, or racial and ethnic relations, let alone Lockheed Martin's involvement in all kinds of secret defense operations, including some whose ethical soundness might be challenged. One wonders how such an ethics program would have fared at Enron or Arthur Andersen.

In the end, whether a person becomes a good worker depends on whether he or she is disposed to carry out good work and willing to keep on trying to achieve that end when the going gets tough. We have found it useful to invoke the four *M*s as signposts toward the achievement of good work.

1. *Mission.* Whether at school, after school, in training, or at the workplace, an individual should specify what she is trying to achieve in her activities—in the terms we've been using, what goals are woven in the fabric of the hat she is wearing. Without an explicit knowledge of one's goals, it is likely that a person will remain directionless or head for trouble.

2. *Models.* It is very important to have exposure—preferably directly or at least through texts or other media—to individuals who themselves embody good work. In the absence of such models, the young worker finds it difficult to know how to proceed. At times, negative role models can also provide needed cautionary tales.

3. *Mirror test—individual version.* The aspiring good worker must from time to time look into the mirror, without squinting, and see whether she is proceeding in ways of which she approves. The question to pose is, "Am I being a good worker—and, if not, what can I do to become one?" Since we are all subject to self-delusion, it is important that other knowledgeable and candid individuals be consulted on this question. Two worthy consultants could be one's own mother ("if she knew everything that I was doing, what would she think?") and the editor of the local newspaper ("if he knew all and printed it, would I be ashamed or proud?").

4. *Mirror test—professional responsibility.* Initially, young workers need to attend to their own souls. Ultimately, however, that is not enough. Even if one is doing good work oneself— for the accounting firm Arthur Andersen or the newspaper the *New York Times* or the law firm Hill and Barlow—that does not suffice if one's colleagues are behaving in ways that are unprofessional. With the assumption of authority and maturity comes the obligation to monitor what our peers are doing and, when necessary, to call them to account. As the seventeenth-century French playwright Jean-Baptiste Molière declared, "We are responsible not only for what we do but for what we do not do."

In our own research, we have been experimenting with various interventions designed to foster ethical work. For midcareer journalists, we have devised a traveling curriculum. Reporters, editors, and publishers collaborate to come up with solutions to genuine problems (e.g., how to provide fair coverage of an issue in which the news outlet has a personal stake) and share the most promising strategies with their colleagues. For leaders of higher education, we have devised measures of the distinctive goals and missions for the various stakeholders, ranging from students to alumni; we are developing ways to help these stakeholders work together synergistically for greater alignment within the institution. And for secondary-school students, we have prepared a toolkit of sample work dilemmas (e.g., what to do when financial support of a student activity depends on kowtowing to a dubious policy of the sponsoring school). Students ponder these dilemmas, discuss possible solutions, and think about how they will behave when they themselves encounter such dilemmas at work, five or ten years hence (see www.goodworkproject.org).

Parents, classroom teachers, and other adults in the neighborhood cannot provide direct guidance to work, because they cannot anticipate the precise jobs that their students will have in the future, let alone the specific dilemma on which the future worker may be impaled. (Note the parallels to disciplinary education, where a student's understanding is most reliably assessed through the administering of unfamiliar problems.) But these individuals can serve as models of ethical workers, generically, and they can help model and mold those ethical stances that should prove useful across a variety of workplaces. Teachers in professional schools and designated mentors have far more relevant knowledge; but often students have only fleeting exposure to these adults, and by that time, they may already have embarked on an ethical or unethical trajectory that is likely to endure through life. Not every young person has the good fortune of living in a community like Reggio Emilia or working at an institution that continues to embody good work.

For all of these reasons, it is especially important that the growing young person himself begin to think in terms of missions, models, and mirrors. To the extent that these considerations become part of his mental architecture (habits of mind), and to the extent that he is prepared to change course when reorientation is indicated, he will be able to assume the principal responsibility for the quality of his work: its excellence, its ethical tenor, its meaningfulness. Constant reflection and wide consultation are in order. And perhaps one day, having been a good worker, he can become a trustee of his profession and his planet. He can help ensure good work in succeeding generations, thereby contributing to the shape of a world in which our descendants would want to live.

In June 2005, I asked the cellist Yo-Yo Ma what he considered to be good work in his role as a leading musical performer. Based on much previous reflection, Ma outlined three distinct obligations: (1) to perform the repertoire as excellently as possible; (2) to be able to work together with other musicians, particularly under conditions where one has to proceed rapidly, and develop the necessary common understandings and trust; (3) to pass on one's knowledge, skills, understanding, and orientation to succeeding generations, so that music as he cherishes it can endure.[22] Coming from someone who himself embodies good work, as much as anyone whom I know, this elegant formulation is especially meaningful.

While developed with reference to the workplace, our analysis lends itself readily to an individual's role as a citizen. Here, again, one sees the necessity of developing the capacity for abstract thought. The aspiring good citizen asks about the mission of her community and how it can best be achieved; the positive and negative role models for membership in the community; the extent to which she can look at herself clearly in the mirror and feel that she has fulfilled the role of citizen; and the way in which she can help foster citizenry among the other members of the community. Perhaps such good citizenship was easier to achieve in the agora of ancient Athens, the piazzas of medieval Bologna, or the small towns of nineteenth-century New England; but the need for such citizenship remains as important today as ever. Moreover, at a time when the United States is calling on other societies to adopt democratic institutions, it behooves us to model an engaged citizenry. Otherwise, advocates of "democracy elsewhere" appear to the rest of the world simply as hypocrites. Good work may begin in the bosom of the individual, but ultimately it must extend to the workplace, the nation, and the global community.

CHAPTER 7

Conclusion

Toward the Cultivation of the Five Minds

THE PROJECT OUTLINED in this book is ambitious, even grandiose. At times, I've felt overwhelmed by the challenge of developing this quintet of minds and then orchestrating their smooth interaction in a person (or a population) who lives in our global world. Yet the effort has seemed worthwhile. It's better for an aim to exceed one's grasp than for one to aim too low or too narrowly.

Now the time has come to take stock—to review the major claims and to clear up some lingering questions. In this book, I've spoken a lot about synthesis. I have not hesitated to praise some syntheses, while expressing reservations about others. And so the challenge of synthesis is in my hands. In the following series of similarly configured boxes, I recapitulate the principal features of each kind of mind. Thereafter, I review some of the obstacles to the formations of these minds, speculate about the order in which these minds might be developed, and then offer suggestions about how the ensemble of minds might best be cultivated.

The Disciplined Mind

Employing the ways of thinking associated with major scholarly disciplines (history, math, science, art, etc.) and major professions (law, medicine, management, finance, etc., as well as crafts and trades); capable of applying oneself diligently, improving steadily, and continuing beyond formal education

> **Examples (formal education).** Mastering of history, mathematics, science, and other key subjects; completing professional training

> **Examples (place of work).** Continuing mastery of one's professional or employment role(s), including the acquisition of additional disciplinary or interdisciplinary acumen

> **Period of development.** Begins before adolescence; continues as lifelong learning

> **Pseudoforms.** Asserting of mastery without a decade or so of practice; following rigidly the letter of procedures without a sense of the purposes and boundaries of the discipline and the areas where thinking needs to be flexible the conventional wisdom is inappropriate; faking one's preparation or performance

The Synthesizing Mind

Selecting crucial information from the copious amounts available; arraying that information in ways that make sense to self and to others

Examples (formal education). Preparing for assignments and tests in school by organizing materials in ways that are helpful to self and others (especially the grader!)

Examples (place of work). Recognizing new information/skills that are important and then incorporating them into one's knowledge base and one's professional repertoire

Period of development. Starts in childhood, under the best of circumstances; becomes more deliberate over time; continues perennially as new knowledge accumulates and needs to be digested and organized

Pseudoforms. Selecting materials in a haphazard way; offering integrations that do not stand up to scrutiny, either by self or by knowledgeable others; inappropriate organizing frameworks; lack of an organizing stance; summaries that feature overly grandiose "lumping" or nitpicking "splitting"

The Creating Mind

Going beyond existing knowledge and syntheses to pose new questions, offer new solutions, fashion works that stretch existing genres or configure new ones; creation builds on one or more established disciplines and requires an informed "field" to make judgments of quality and acceptability

Examples (formal education). Going beyond class requirements to pose new questions; coming up with unexpected but appropriate school products and projects

Examples (place of work). Thinking outside the box—putting forth recommendations for new practices and products, explicating them, seeking endorsement and enactment; for leader, formulating and pursuing new visions

Period of development. Robust personality begins to develop early—informed challenges to orthodoxy await at least partial mastery of disciplined and synthesizing thinking

Pseudoforms. Offering apparent innovations that are either superficial variations of long-existing knowledge or sharp departures that may be novel but are not accepted ultimately by the knowledgeable field

The Respectful Mind

Responding sympathetically and constructively to differences among individuals and among groups; seeking to understand and work with those who are different; extending beyond mere tolerance and political correctness

Examples (formal education). Seeking to understand and work effectively with peers, teachers, and staff, whatever their backgrounds and viewpoints

Examples (place of work). Working effectively with peers, supervisors, employees, irrespective of their backgrounds and status; developing capacity for forgiveness

Period of development. Supportive environment should be present from birth; at school, work, in the media, role models (positive and negative, recognized as such) are crucial

Pseudoforms. Exhibiting mere tolerance, without any effort to understand or work smoothly with others; paying homage to those with more power and status while deprecating, dismissing, ridiculing or ignoring those with less power; behaving reflexively toward an entire group, without attending to the qualities of specific individual

The Ethical Mind

Abstracting crucial features of one's role at work and one's role as a citizen and acting consistently with those conceptualizations; striving toward good work and good citizenship

Examples (formal education). Reflecting on one's role as a student or as a future professional and attempting to fulfill that role appropriately and responsibly

Examples (place of work). Knowing the core values of one's profession and seeking to maintain them and pass them on, even at times of rapid and unpredictable change; with maturity, adopting the role of the trustee, who assumes stewardship of a domain and is willing to speak out even at personal cost; recognizing one's responsibilities as a citizen of one's community, region, nation, and world, and acting on those responsibilities

Period of development. Awaits the time when an individual can think conceptually, abstractly, about the role of a worker and of a citizen; acting in an ethical way presupposes strength of character; may require supportive relations of a horizontal and vertical sort, as well as periodic inoculations

Pseudoforms. Expounding a good, responsible line but failing to embody that course in one's own actions; practicing ethics in a small arena while acting irresponsibly in the larger sphere (or vice versa); compromising on what is proper in the short run or over the long haul

RESISTANCES AND OBSTACLES

Even if my conception of five minds for the future is on the mark, it will scarcely be easy to achieve. People are loath to alter practices with which they were raised and with which they are now all too comfortable. Resistances and obstacles are likely to assume various forms:

- *Conservatism.* We are doing perfectly fine with traditional education and longstanding practices at work—why change?

- *Faddism.* Visionaries and pundits are always calling for something new. Why should we believe that these five minds are any better than earlier calls for other forms of mind?

- *Hidden risks.* Who knows the hidden costs of this regimen? Perhaps excessive creativity will slip into anarchy. Perhaps naive or misplaced respectfulness will make us sitting ducks for terrorists.

- *Impotence.* These goals sound good. But I don't know how to achieve them, and I won't know how to evaluate whether they're actually being realized. Show me what to do, and don't expect me just to assent.

Anyone who seeks to develop minds must take time to ferret out and attempt to understand such resistances. But as a general rule, one is ill advised to confront the resistances directly; such a step typically engenders defensiveness. It makes more sense to begin with areas where a target group feels unsatisfied or frustrated and to suggest ways in which felt deficits, problems, or frustrations can be counteracted. So, for example, if there has been a lot of conflict recently in a classroom or a boardroom, a concern with respect is more likely to gain a sympathetic audience. Or if jobs in the region are being lost due to outsourcing, and the most capable residents are taking high-tech jobs elsewhere, a focus on the creating mind may become timely.

Those who appear open to change need exposure to models—individuals as well as institutions—that exemplify the desired changes. Sometimes, these models can be paragons—examples whom the advocates may not know personally but whom they can admire from afar. The biologist E. O. Wilson can serve as an example of the synthesizing mind; the dancer Martha Graham exemplifies the creative mind; the environmentalist Rachel Carson illustrates the ethical mind. But the most effective examples are individuals who are known personally and who—while not immune from human foibles—regularly exhibit key features of the desired roles.

These exemplary figures should present a sharply chiseled view of the desired traits. A disciplined person should embody the ways of thinking and acting that distinguish her chosen discipline(s) and not just spew forth a lot of heterogeneous knowledge about the subject. A synthesizer should put ideas together in a way that is cogent and replicable, and not merely offer a convenient or cute package. A creating mind should be both original *and* appropriate—sheer novelty or eccentricity or instant celebrity does not suffice. A respectful mind should transcend mere tolerance, displaying active interest in and affection for those who look different, including those of lower status. An ethical mind must comport itself in ways that support the broader profession and the wider society—even, or especially, when those actions go against one's narrow self-interest.

Needless to say, the ambient society does not always support the propagation of such positive role models. It is difficult to be a disciplined thinker when television quiz shows lavishly reward disparate factual knowledge. It is difficult to be respectful toward others when an "argument mentality" characterizes politics and the mass media, and when bald-faced intimidators morph into cultural heroes. It is difficult to behave ethically when so many rewards—

monetary and renown—are showered on those who spurn ethics but have not, or at least have not yet, been held accountable by the broader society. Were our media and our leaders to honor the five kinds of minds foregrounded here, and to ostracize those who violate these virtues, the job of educators and supervisors would be incalculably easier.

AN ORDER FOR MASTERING THE MINDS?

Let's say, then, that resistances have been muted and a supportive atmosphere has been created. Is there an optimal order in which to introduce these kinds of minds?

I question whether one should first focus on one kind of mind and then the next, in lockstep fashion. (In this way, I differ from educator Benjamin Bloom, with whom I am sometimes compared.)[1] I find it preferable to conceptualize the five kinds of minds in epigenetic fashion. That is, the full range of minds are in the picture in incipient form from the first, but each steps into the spotlight during a specific period of development. (In this way, I resemble my teacher, psychologist Erik Erikson, who introduced the idea of epigenesis in psychological development.)[2] With that stipulation, here are four comments about timing:

1. *Respect.* From the beginning, one must begin by creating a respectful atmosphere toward others. In the absence of civility, other educational goals prove infinitely harder to achieve. Instances of disrespect must be labeled as such; each must be actively discouraged and its practitioners ostracized.

   (An aside on literacy: the first cognitive assignment for all schools is mastery of the basic literacies of reading, writing, and calculation. Because this point is and has long been uncontroversial, I need not elaborate on it here.)

2. *Discipline.* Once one has become literate, by the end of the elementary years, the time is at hand for the acquisition of the major scholarly ways of thinking—at a minimum, scientific, mathematical, historical, artistic. Each takes years to inculcate, and so delays are costly.

3. *Synthesis.* Equipped with major disciplinary ways of thinking, the student is poised to make judicious kinds of syntheses and, as appropriate, to engage in interdisciplinary thinking.

4. *Ethics.* During the years of secondary school and college, one becomes capable of abstract, distanced thinking. One can now conceptualize the world of work and the responsibilities of the citizen and acts on those conceptualizations.

Even the ordering is, at best, rough and ready—very far from a logical or psychological sequencing. Note that I have not placed *creativity* at a specific place in this sequence. An emphasis on creativity in formal education depends on its place in the broader society. In a society like the United States, where creativity is honored in the media and on the streets, there is less of an imperative to focus on creative uses of mind in formal scholastic settings. In societies that are more traditional, an early emphasis on creativity becomes important in schools.

In any event, creativity goes hand in glove with disciplinary thinking. In the absence of relevant disciplines, it is not possible to be genuinely creative. In the absence of creativity, disciplines can be used only to rehearse the status quo. Moreover, creativity itself has different facets. The personality of the creative individual—robust, risk taking, resilient—needs to be cultivated from early on; but apt challenging of disciplinary thinking awaits at least a rough-and-ready mastery of that discipline.

Even the later emerging forms of mind can be anticipated. For example, while ethical thinking proves difficult before adolescence, it is never too early to model reflection on the advantages and disadvantages of various courses of action, or the wisdom of attending to the opinions of others. Cultivation of these dispositions from an early age smooths the way for later ethical discourse and decision making. Younger persons may benefit from family or classroom discussions of ethical issues, even if they cannot completely follow the logic or abstractness of individual contributions.

No doubt schools, regions, and societies will differ from one another in their emphases on the various kinds of minds, and in the order in which they highlight those minds. Such variations are appropriate and, indeed, welcome. For example, we scarcely know enough to declare with confidence that synthesizing comes before or after creating. Moreover, it is likely that individuals—and perhaps groups or even entire societies—will emerge as stronger in one form than in another.

THE FIVE MINDS AND THE FUTURE

One point stands out. Whatever their importance in times past, these five minds are likely to be crucial in a world marked by the hegemony of science and technology, global transmission of huge amounts of information, handling of routine tasks by computers and robots, and ever increasing contacts of all sorts between diverse populations. Those who succeed in cultivating the pentad of minds are most likely to thrive.

Ideally, of course, teachers, trainers, and supervisors should cherish and embody these kinds of minds. In reality, however, many individuals in positions of influence will themselves be deficient in one or more kinds of minds; indeed, if my own analysis is correct, as a society we have been until recently relatively blind to the importance of these minds. (A focus on subject matter information, standardized testing, and the often arbitrary conventions of the school day may even desensitize us to the need for such minds.) That situation can only be rectified if, in the future, the training of teachers and other kinds of leaders prioritizes the skills and dispositions entailed in each kind of mind.

How does one know that one is making progress in achieving each of these minds? The answer seems self-evident, and yet it must be stated bluntly: anyone who aims to cultivate these minds must have a concept of what it means to be successful and what it means to fail. It is always prudent to aim for reasonable targets: the young musician or mathematician or marketer should be a better disciplinarian or synthesizer at the end of the year than at the beginning; but improvements will differ between individuals, and periods of stasis or regression can be anticipated. The nurturer needs to have in mind what *better* means, so that both she and her student can critique successive efforts in terms of relevant criteria. The effective pedagogue—whether she's a third grade teacher or the leader of a SWAT team—needs to be cognizant of the resistances and how best to counter them. And both she and her students need to be wary of the pseudoversions that may emerge and that will look, to the uninitiated, like genuine instances of discipline, synthesis, creation, respect, and ethics.

In no sense need these kinds of minds represent a zero-sum. There is no legitimate reason why the cultivation of one kind of mind should preclude the cultivation of others. Yet, as a practical matter, there may be tradeoffs. Too great a focus on discipline may impede creativity; if you come to accept all of the strictures of a discipline, you may be loath or even unable to deviate from them. As a related example, there may also be a tension between respect and creativity. Creativity requires that one be willing to challenge the orthodoxy; but what happens when your beloved mentor embodies that orthodoxy? There may at times be a tension between respect and ethics. An ethical stance may require you to distance yourself from an offending peer, whom you have sought to treat in a respectful manner. Or, as epitomized in the example of Lincoln, one's designated role may dictate a course of action that is repugnant on a personal basis. As they mature, individuals need to be alert to these tensions so that they do not find themselves flummoxed.

It is up to the educational system as a whole—the educational system in the broadest sense—to ensure that the ensemble of minds is cultivated. In one sense, this is a job of synthesis—making sure that all five kinds of minds are developed. But equally, it is an ethical obligation: in the years ahead, societies will not survive—let alone thrive—unless as citizens we respect and cultivate the quintet of minds valorized here. When I speak of the "broadest sense" of education, I have in mind that schools alone cannot do the job. The burden of education must be shared by parents, neighbors, the traditional and digital media, the church, and other communal institutions. Moreover, societies will differ in the division of responsibilities for the cultivation of such minds. Thus, respect can be nurtured at home, at school, and/or on the street; the mass media may model disciplinary thinking in one society, interdisciplinarity in a second society, or undisciplined thinking in a third. When one party does not participate, others must pick up the ball. When one party (say, the media) sets a bad example, then other parties (say, parents and religious leaders) must compensate. And in those regrettable cases where none of these entities assumes its share, the responsibility almost inevitably falls on the schools—an unreasonable state of affairs.

Of course, the educational imperative transcends the school years. The workplace, the professions, the leaders and foot soldiers of civic society must all do their part—and that obligation cannot be spurned or postponed or fobbed off on institutions that are incapable of picking up the responsibility. Optimally, of course, the shrewd manager or leader selects individuals who already possess these minds; then the challenge is to maintain them, sharpen them, catalyze them to work together, offer them as role models for future recruits. Few executives are so fortunate, however. When one has hired an individual who proves deficient in one or more of these kinds of minds, the options are clear:

1. Separate the person from the organization as expeditiously as possible. A person incapable of respect or prone to unethical acts can quickly poison an entire division.

2. Assign that individual to a niche where the deficiency poses no threat to the organization. For example, not every worker needs to be a synthesizer or a creator.

3. Make it clear to the worker that he needs to improve with respect to one or more of these competences. Model the desired behavior, and point to clear positive (and negative) models. Create a positive, trusting atmosphere. Set reasonable goals. Provide regular, pointed feedback. If progress is made, rejoice. If progress is not forthcoming, revert to options 1 or 2. And if you find that many of your employees are deficient in a kind of mind, reflect on your recruiting procedure, the ethos of the institution, your own example, and your own teaching.

As I consider educational, political, and managerial systems that might actually nurture these five kinds of minds, I gain confidence that our positive human potentials can be cultivated. Disciplines, syntheses, and creativity can be put to all kinds of ends, including nefarious ones; but such perversion is much less likely if we have also cultivated a sense of respect and an ethical orientation. The five kinds of minds can and should work synergistically.

We might deem as wise the person in the society who cultivates these minds in timely fashion and deploys each when and where it is most needed. Here, again, the preeminence of goals and values must be stressed: an educational system is not worthy of its name unless its representatives can clearly articulate what that system is striving to achieve and what it seeks to avoid or curtail. It may be the case that computers can achieve literacy and a measure of disciplined thinking. But as we move toward the skills of synthesizing and creating, we move toward realms that are—and may well remain—distinctively human. And at least on my analysis, the terms *respect* and *ethics* only make sense within a community of vital but vulnerable human beings—to refer to a mechanical device, no matter how fast and byte-laden, as "respectful" or "ethical" is to commit a category error.

Perhaps members of the human species will not be prescient enough to survive, or perhaps it will take far more immediate threats to our survival before we make common cause with our fellow human beings. In any event the survival and thriving of our species will depend on our nurturing of potentials that are distinctly human.

Notes

Chapter 1

1. Howard Gardner, *The Mind's New Science: The History of the Cognitive Revolution* (New York: Basic Books, 1985).

2. Howard Gardner, *Frames of Mind: The Theory of Multiple Intelligences* (1983; repr., New York: Basic Books, 2004).

3. John Rawls, *A Theory of Justice* (Cambridge, MA: Harvard University Press, 1971).

4. "The Battle for Brainpower," *The Economist*, October 7 2006, 3.

5. See Jagdish Bhagwati, *In Defense of Globalization* (New York: Oxford University Press, 2005); Thomas Friedman, *The World Is Flat* (New York: Farrar, Straus and Giroux, 2005); and Marcelo Suarez-Orozco and Desiree Qin-Hilliard, *Globalization and Education* (Berkeley, CA: University of California Press, 2004).

Chapter 2

1. Alan Bennett, *The History Boys* (London: Faber & Faber, 2004).

2. Lee S. Shulman, "Signature Pedagogies," *Daedalus*, Summer 2005, 52–59.

3. David Perkins, "Education for the Unknown" (paper presented at Harvard Project Zero, Cambridge, MA, March 5, 2006).

4. Donald Schön, *The Reflective Practitioner* (New York: Basic Books, 1983).

5. Arthur Rubinstein, *My Many Years* (New York: Knopf, 1980), 218–219, 258.

6. Michael Maccoby, personal communication, October 11 2006.

Chapter 3

1. Severs's comments from personal communication, August 29, 2006.

2. Gerald Holton, *Thematic Origins of Scientific Thought* (Cambridge, MA: Harvard University Press, 1988).

3. Clayton Christensen, *The Innovator's Dilemma* (New York: Harper Business, 1997).

4. Jim Collins, *Good to Great and the Social Sectors* (Boulder, CO: Jim Collins, 2005).

5. Peter Galison, *Einstein's Clocks, Poincaré's Maps: Empires of Time* (New York: Norton, 2004).

6. Bill Bryson, *A Short History of Nearly Everything* (New York: Broadway, 2003), 1.

7. Ibid., 476.

8. Ken Wilber, *A Brief History of Everything* (Boston: Shambhala, 1996), 16.

9. Ken Wilber, *The Essential Ken Wilber* (Boston: Shambhala, 1998), 7.

10. Wilber, *A Brief History of Everything*, 42.

11. Ibid., 72–73.

12. Wilber, *The Essential Ken Wilber,* 113.

13. C. P. Snow, *The Search* (London: Penguin, 1950), 243.

14. John Gardner (1912–2002) was an outstanding American public servant. We were not related.

15. Steven Johnson, "Tool for Thought," *New York Times Book Review*, January 30, 2005, end piece.

16. Richard Light, *Making the Most of College* (Cambridge, MA: Harvard University Press, 2001).

17. Edward O. Wilson, *Consilience* (New York: Knopf, 1998).

18. Vartan Gregorian, "Colleges Must Reconstruct the Unity of Knowledge," *Chronicle of Higher Education*, June 4, 2004, B-12.

19. Quoted in David Remnick, "The Wanderer," *The New Yorker*, September 18, 2006, 65.

Chapter 4

1. Edward de Bono, *Lateral Thinking* (New York: Harper, 1973).

2. Mihaly Csikszentmihalyi, *Creativity* (New York: Harper Collins, 1996).

3. John Maynard Keynes, *The General Theory of Employment, Interest, and Money* (1936; repr., New York: Prometheus, 1977).

4. Quoted in Howard Gardner, *Artful Scribbles* (New York: Basic Books, 1982) 8.

5. Howard Gardner, *To Open Minds: Chinese Clues to the Dilemma of American Education* (New York: Basic Books, 1989).

6. Teresa Amabile, *How to Kill Creativity* (Boston: Harvard Business School Press, 2000).

7. Bethany McLean and Peter Elkind, *The Smartest Guys in the Room* (New York: Viking, 2004).

8. Jeffrey Immelt, "Growth as a Process: The HBR Interview," *Harvard Business Review*, June 2006.

9. Gary Taubes, *Bad Science: The Short Life and Weird Times of Cold Fusion* (New York: Random House, 1993), xviii.

10. Ibid., 112.

11. Such books include J. R. Huizenga, *Cold Fusion: The Scientific Farce of the Century* (New York: Oxford University Press, 1994); Eugene F. Mallove, *Fire from Ice: Searching for the Truth Behind the Cold Fusion Furor* (New York: John Wiley, 1991); Bart Simon, *Undead Science* (New Brunswick, NJ: Rutgers University Press, 2002); and Taubes, *Bad Science*.

12. Richard Florida, *The Rise of the Creative Class* (New York: Basic Books, 2003).

13. Bill Joy, *Why the Future Doesn't Need Us: How 21st Century Technologies Threaten to Make Humans an Endangered Species* (New York: Random House Audio, 2006).

Chapter 5

1. Michael Balter, "First Jewelry? Old Shell Beads Suggest Early Use of Symbols," *Science* 23, no. 5781 (2006): 1731.

2. W. H. Auden, "September 1, 1939."

3. Margaret Talbot, "The Baby Lab: How Elizabeth Spelke Peers into the Infant Mind," *The New Yorker*, September 4, 2006.

4. Vivian Paley, *You Can't Say You Can't Play* (Cambridge, MA: Harvard University Press, 1993).

5. Yarrow Dunham, A. S. Baron, and M. R. Banaji, "From American City to Japanese Village: A Cross-Cultural Investigation of Implicit Race Attitudes," *Child Development* (forthcoming).

6. Sara Lawrence-Lightfoot, *Respect* (New York: Perseus Books, 1999).

7. James Atlas, *Bellow: A Biography* (New York: Modern Library, 2002), 574.

8. Robert Payne, *The Life and Death of Mahatma Gandhi* (1969; repr. New York: Dutton, 1995), 412.

9. Niall Ferguson, *Empire* (New York: Penguin, 2004), 335.

10. Amy Edmondson, R. Bohmer, and G. Pisano, "Speeding Up Team Learning," *Harvard Business Review*, October 2001.

11. David Garvin and Michael Roberts, "What You Don't Know About Making Decisions," *Harvard Business Review*, September 2001.

12. John Seely Brown, "Towards Respectful Organization" in *Organizations as Knowledge Systems*, ed. Haridimos Tsoukas and Nikolaos Myolonopoulus (Houndmills, UK: Palgrave Macmillan, 2003).

13. Rodney Kramer, "The Great Intimidators," *Harvard Business Review*, February 2006.

14. Samuel Oliner, *Altruistic Personality* (New York: Touchstone, 1992).

15. Daniel Barenboim and Edward W. Said, *Parallels and Paradoxes: Explorations in Music and Society* (New York: Pantheon, 2002), 6, 10, 11.

16. Alan Riding, "Harmony Across the Divide," *New York Times*, August 20, 2006, Arts and Leisure, 1.

17. Ibid.

18. See www.silkroadproject.org/press/faq.html.

19. See Rudy Govier and Wilhelm Verwoerd, "Trust and the Problem of National Reconciliation," *Philosophy of the Social Sciences* 32, no. 3 (2002): 187–205; Priscilla B. Hayner, "Fifteen Truth Commissions, 1974–1994: A Comparative Study," *Human Rights Quarterly* 16, no. 4 (1994): 597–655; Charles O. Lerche, "Truth Commissions and National Reconciliation: Some Reflections on Theory and Practice," http://www.gmu.edu/academic/pcs/LERCHE71PCS.html; and Martha Minow, *Between Vengeance and Forgiveness: Facing History After Genocide and Mass Violence* (Boston: Beacon Press, 1998).

20. Lerche, "Truth Commissions and National Reconciliation."

21. Minow, *Between Vengeance and Forgiveness*.

Chapter 6

1. Howard Gardner, Mihaly Csikszentmihalyi, and William Damon, *Good Work: When Excellence and Ethics Meet* (New York: Basic Books, 2001). Online at www.goodworkproject.org.

2. "The Ten Best Schools in the World and What We Can Learn from Them," *Newsweek*, December 2, 1991, 50–59.

3. Robert Putnam, Robert Leonardi, and Raffaella Nanetti, *Making Democracy Work* (Princeton, NJ: Princeton University Press, 1994).

4. Carolyn Edwards, Lella Gandini, and George Forman, eds., *The Hundred Languages of Children* (Norwood, NJ: Ablex, 1993). Harvard Project Zero, *Making Learning Visible* (Reggio Emilia, Italy: Reggio Children Publishers, 2001).

5. Judith Rich Harris, *The Nurture Assumption* (New York: Free Press, 1999).

6. Wendy Fischman, Becca Solomon, Deborah Greenspan, and Howard Gardner, *Making Good: How Young People Cope with Moral Dilemmas at Work* (Cambridge, MA: Harvard University Press, 2004).

7. Transcript of interview with Steve Skowron, transmitted to author June 10, 2005.

8. Compare this stance with John Hasnas, *Trapped: When Acting Ethically Is Against the Law* (Washington DC: Cato Institute, 2006).

9. Quoted in Peter J. Dougherty, *Who's Afraid of Adam Smith? How the Market Lost Its Soul* (New York: Wiley, 2002), 6.

10. Ibid., frontispiece; J. Sacks, *To Heal a Fractured World: The Ethics of Responsibility* (New York: Shocken), 2005.

11. Elizabeth Kolbert, *New Yorker*, June 30, 2002.

12. Paula Marshall, "Facing the Storm: The Closing of a Great Form" (paper prepared for the GoodWork Project, Cambridge, MA, 2004).

13. Debbie Freier, "Compromised Work in the Public Accounting Profession: The Issue of Independence" (paper prepared for the GoodWork Project, Cambridge, MA, 2004).

14. Bethany McLean and Peter Elkind, *The Smartest Guys in the Room* (New York: Viking, 2004).

15. G. William Dauphinais and Colin Price, eds., *Straight from the CEO* (New York: Simon and Schuster, 1998), 257.

16. Quoted in "Summer Jobs," *New Yorker*, July 4, 2005, 30.

17. Peter Singer, *Practical Ethics* (New York: Cambridge University Press, 1999).

18. Albert O. Hirschman, *Exit, Voice, and Loyalty* (Cambridge MA: Harvard University Press, 1970).

19. Quoted in Ronald White, *The Eloquent President* (New York: Random House, 2005), 150.

20. White, *The Eloquent President,* 260.

21. Daniel Terris, *Ethics at Work* (Waltham, MA: Brandeis University Press, 2005).

22. Yo-Yo Ma, personal communication with the author, June 23, 2005.

Chapter 7

1. Benjamin Bloom, *Taxonomy of Educational Objectives* (New York: Longmans, Green, and Co., 1956).

2. Erik H. Erikson, *Childhood and Society* (New York: Norton, 1963).

Index

About the Author

Howard Gardner is the John H. and Elisabeth A. Hobbs Professor of Cognition and Education at the Harvard Graduate School of Education. He also holds positions as Adjunct Professor of Psychology at Harvard University and Senior Director of Harvard Project Zero.

Gardner is best known in educational circles for his theory of multiple intelligences, a critique of the notion that there exists but a single human intelligence that can be assessed by standard psychometric instruments. For over two decades, he and colleagues at Project Zero have been working on the design of performance-based assessments; education for understanding; the use of multiple intelligences to achieve more personalized curriculum, instruction, and assessment; and the nature of interdisciplinary efforts in education. Since 1995, in collaboration with psychologists Mihaly Csikszentmihalyi and William Damon, Gardner has studied GoodWork—work that is at once excellent in quality, personally engaging. and socially responsible. Building on over 1,200 in depth interviews in 9 professions, the GoodWork project is now disseminating key insights to students and young professionals.

Gardner is the author of several hundred articles and two dozen books translated into twenty-six languages, including *Changing Minds:*

The Art and Science of Changing Our Own and Other People's Minds;
Good Work: When Excellence and Ethics Meet; *The Disciplined Mind: Beyond Facts and Standardized Tests, The K–12 Education That Every Child Deserves*; *Multiple Intelligences: New Horizons*; *The Development and Education of the Mind*; and *Making Good: How Young People Cope with Moral Dilemmas at Work* (with Wendy Fischman, Becca Solomon, and Deborah Greenspan).

Among numerous honors, Gardner received a MacArthur Prize Fellowship in 1981. In 1990, he was the first American to receive the University of Louisville's Grawemeyer Award in Education, and in 2000 he received a Fellowship from the John S. Guggenheim Memorial Foundation. He has received honorary degrees from twenty-one colleges and universities, including institutions in Ireland, Italy, Israel, and Chile. He is a member of the American Philosophical Association, the American Academy of Arts and Sciences, and the National Academy of Education.